The Way to Write Magazine Articles

For over thirty years, John Hines has been writing articles for a wide range of general magazines and, in addition, specialising in writing for the medical, industrial management and natural history fields.

Together with his wife, Molly, he lectures extensively on creative writing courses and at writers' workshops. He is a lecturer participating in the 'Writers on Tour' scheme run by the Welsh Arts Council and the Regional Arts Associations.

John Hines lives in Gwent.

By the same author:

The Way to Write Non-fiction

The Way to Write Magazine Articles

JOHN HINES

Elm Tree Books . London

ELM TREE BOOKS

Published by the Penguin Group
Penguin Books Ltd, 27 Wrights Lane, London W8 5TZ, England
Penguin Books USA Inc., 375 Hudson Street, New York, New York 10014, USA
Penguin Books Australia Ltd, Ringwood, Victoria, Australia
Penguin Books Canada Ltd, 10 Alcorn Avenue, Toronto, Ontario, Canada M4V 3B2
Penguin Books (NZ) Ltd, 182–190 Wairau Road, Auckland 10, New Zealand

Penguin Books Ltd, Registered Offices: Harmondsworth, Middlesex, England

First published in Great Britain 1987 by
Elm Tree Books/Hamish Hamilton Ltd
3 5 7 9 10 8 6 4

Printed in England by Clays Ltd, St Ives plc

For my dear wife, Molly, in appreciation of her gentle encouragement, her tolerance of my untidy writing methods and her unselfishness in pretending that my writing is more important than her own

Contents

Chapter One

The first steps

I never had the advantage of learning my journalism in a newspaper office. My professional journalist friends tell me it is a hard world, but it is one in which you learn fast. I tell them that it is a darn sight harder to learn in isolation, without the discipline of deadlines, the goad of supervision, the threat of the sack and the occasional word of encouragement.

Having started from scratch with no guidance, I can appreciate the lot of most beginners, their often total ignorance, the loneliness of working alone and the crushing depression of repeated rejection. I also remember the sweet taste of success – like that first cheque I would have dearly loved to frame, but couldn't afford to.

Remembering these beginnings, I have set out, quite unashamedly, to try to teach you how to make money from writing magazine articles. You don't have to be brilliant in any respect to write saleable material. There is no magic formula. All you need is perseverance and the willingness to work within the broad guidelines of this book. If you have the ability to write reasonable English, then you should be able to write and sell articles.

But it would be wrong to assume that saleability is incompatible with fine writing. There is no reason why an article should not show a sensitive use of words and all the other desirable facets of the writer's skill – no reason, that is, except the dictates of the market.

Between the beginner and publication there are both stepping-stones and pitfalls. Although I discovered many of them the hard way, I must give credit to the knowledge and skills of those writer and journalist friends, without whose guidance my journey would have been harder and much less successful.

In my early days I wrote a little poetry, started and abandoned a novel and played around at writing generally. I never saw myself as a real writer. I started it seriously from the basest of motives – money.

It was suggested to me that I should write a book on the making of some unique fishing-lures I had designed. I was hard-up and decided that, although the subject would hardly warrant a book, it might make an article.

My article must have been one of the most appallingly presented pieces of writing which ever landed on that unfortunate editor's desk. Yet it obviously said something which attracted him. After much sub-editing, he published it and sent me seven guineas. That was over thirty years ago and seven guineas was a significant sum – enough to set me off hunting feverishly for something else to write about.

I had designed and built a rocking-horse for the children. It was novel, easy to make, safe and cheap. I wrote a short article and the same editor took it and paid me four guineas.

I believed that I was now a writer and, as long as the ideas flowed, I could go on making money. I even thought I might give up work and write full-time. Unfortunately, it didn't happen like that.

I had realised that the payment was directly proportional to the length of the article. So the next one was to be a big one. I aimed at about ten guineas-worth.

It resulted in my first rejection-slip. It was a shattering experience, sharpened by my early success and my new over-confidence. Unable to bear the humiliation, I stopped writing.

It must have been a year before I wrote again. This time I am sure it was an urge to write, not merely to make money. I scraped together the price of a correspondence course on journalism. The lessons were tedious, the tutor's comments terse and often irrelevant. I finally gave it up as a waste of time, but not before I had discovered the need for market research and the necessity for presenting a typescript in a reasonable way.

My next few efforts brought more rejection slips, but I had now invested hard cash in writing and there was no way I would give up until I had recovered it.

Acceptances came slowly. When they did, I was spurred on to greater effort. I increased my output and at last I was making money.

Modest success stayed with me until I went to the Writers' Summer School, Swanwick, for the first time. It was a revelation. Thanks to my good friend Jill Dick of the *Manchester Evening News*, I discovered how a professional typescript should really look. I was introduced to those little tips which sort out the amateurs from the professionals. Numerous other friends generously guided my stumbling footsteps into the paths of professionalism.

I wrote short-stories at a prodigious rate and sold them like hot cakes. I extended to 12,000 word two-parters and started thinking about serials and even novels. Then, strangely, I became bored with fiction. I realised that I was really a non-fiction writer and that was what I should have been doing all the time.

I worked hard at writing. I got up at 5.30 am to put in work before leaving for my office. I talked to writers. I read a great deal. I used all the skills I could muster to produce good sound material. I improved my photography. I decided on a sales strategy which boosted my success rate considerably. I never missed a Writers' Summer School.

My wife, Molly, is also a writer. Slower and more self-critical than I am, her small output has a perfection which I admire, but can't imitate.

We found that we could help other beginners, who were eager to follow our footsteps. I wrote articles on writing technique. I gave lectures. Together, we tutored residential courses on writing. Our students had successes which proved to us that we were on the right track.

In the last four years, we have received only two rejections. These were recent. Both were mine and at least one was well-deserved. I learnt from them and I shall, with shame, confess about them later in the book.

We have proved from our residential courses, and from the success of our students, that article-writing can be taught, and even for the complete beginner, our blueprint really works. For the more experienced writer, it greatly increases the success rate.

Undoubtedly, there are more would-be writers in the world than ever before. It is proved by the mushrooming of Writers' Circles and writing courses. Most editors' desks are almost submerged under the daily avalanche of unsolicited manuscripts from aspiring writers. Sadly, only a tiny percentage of them ever appear in print. Editors tell me that the vast majority are totally unsuitable and that the writers have no idea of basic editorial requirements.

The pathway to success
The pathway to successful publication is deceptively simple. You need the ability to present a manuscript in a professional manner. The content must be interesting and well constructed. It must be aimed precisely at the magazine's requirements.

All this can be taught quite simply. Competence in these aspects alone will bring some success. Mastery of them will sell a lot of articles. Although you will have the edge on many writers, competition is still fierce and few of us can hope to achieve that brilliant sparkle which might make our work quite irresistible. Ideally, we need something extra and, for me, that means a good sales strategy.

Another possible weapon in our armoury against the competition is the ability to produce simple photographic illustrations. They are by no means essential, but they help, and they also mean you get paid twice.

This book, however, does cater for those who wish to write, yet have no interest in illustrations. It caters for photographers who would like to sell their photographs and realise that they can do so more easily by adding the written word. It will have special value for those who wish to write articles and are prepared to take simple photographs to illustrate them.

4

It is not a book about highflown literature and impeccable grammar. It is about the basic 'nuts and bolts' of writing articles – articles which are readable, satisfying to both writer and reader, but above all, saleable.

Writing is a fascinating craft. It draws on talents we hardly knew we possessed and it develops them. It can give us an emotional outlet. It is both demanding and therapeutic. It stretches our imagination and our horizons. It leads us into fascinating worlds of research, gives us satisfaction and our early successes bring us no little pride. It also teaches us humility, for nothing brings an established writer to earth more smartly than a well-deserved rejection slip.

Motivation

It is worthwhile for beginners to indulge in a little honest introspection and to try to analyse their motivation for writing. Is it the self-satisfaction of seeing yourself in print? Do you want an interesting hobby which might earn you a little pin-money? Do you see writing as a therapy – an introduction to a fantasy world in which you can forget the harsh realities of life? Do you need the money and have few other talents? Is it that you feel a love of words, a satisfaction from self-expression and a burning desire to write?

Self-analysis is difficult and your motivation, like mine, will probably change with time. However, it is useful to have some idea of your purpose in writing, for this could well decide your priorities and your writing strategies.

Whatever your motivation, if you read this book, practise its techniques conscientiously and work diligently, you should cut your rejections to a minimum and it will be most surprising if you are not selling articles consistently in a very short time.

Chapter Two

The article market today

First of all, let us take a brief look at the market place for articles.

Have you noticed how the magazine shelves of the big chain bookshops have gradually extended in recent years? New magazines are being launched all the time. It is true that some of them fail after a couple of issues, but the overall trend is still upwards. According to the current *Willing's Press Guide* there are now over 11,000 magazines and newspapers in circulation. This is obviously to our benefit, for most of these magazines have some potential for the reasonably competent freelance.

Factual articles and 'think' pieces
The dictionary says that an article is 'a literary composition dealing with a particular subject, forming part of a newspaper or magazine.'

Writers see articles in a rather different light. True, there are 'literary' articles, those rather erudite pieces, but writers tend to talk about 'factual articles,' 'think-pieces,' 'shorts,' 'short-shorts' and 'fillers.'

Factual articles are, as one would suppose, based on facts. The facts can come from research or experience – 'Building a rockery from scratch,' 'Restoring our canals,' 'The tragedy of Culloden Moor,' for example.

Think-pieces range from homespun philosophy to outbursts on a favourite hobby-horse – 'Is marriage dead?,' 'Why not restore capital punishment?,' 'Schoolgirl mothers.'

Think-pieces often pose questions which the writer then goes on to answer. Unfortunately, unless the writer is well-known, or an expert, or has something really original to say, perhaps based on unique personal experience, the editor will not be interested. Straightforward think-pieces can be notoriously difficult to sell.

However, there is no clear dividing line between factual articles and think-pieces. Factual articles give the well-informed writer the opportunity to venture opinions. Suitably done it can improve a piece, but overdone it can kill it.

Personal experience can combine facts, feelings and opinions together nicely. This particularly applies to emotional pieces, much loved by some women's magazines – 'Why I gave my baby away,' 'My husband in Pentonville,' 'I was the other woman.'

Shorts

There is no need to worry about the terms 'shorts' and 'short-shorts.' Their length is never clearly defined and we all have different ideas about them. Shorts are generally about 500-750 words. Short-shorts are around 200-400. Having said that, I know one American magazine which considers up to 2,000 words to be a short-short.

Fillers are very brief items, scraps of news, comments, anecdotes, even poems. Readers' letters come into the same broad category. The latter earn a few pounds with, perhaps, £10 for the star letter. Some writers seem to specialise in them, but for most writers the rejections must be high, the earnings lean and the satisfaction small. If you aspire to be a writer, I suggest that you concentrate on articles.

Writers also talk about features or feature articles. This is a loose description generally referring to an important article. The length is usually irrelevant. Quite often the feature will have a mention on the front cover of the magazine. However, these are often merely to catch the eye of the potential purchaser and are no guide to the article's merit. It may also have been mentioned as a forthcoming attraction in the previous issue.

Most articles fall into the 800-2,000 word slot, although

7

some magazines do carry much longer pieces. The most common length of all is about 1,000 words.

Don't let yourself be constrained by thinking of articles by either definition or length. See them only as articles, the length being tailored to the needs of the specific magazine. Apart from the magazines in the newsagents there are other markets for articles which you should consider. Newspapers carry articles. Local newspapers are always on the look-out for interesting pieces, but they generally pay poorly or not at all. National newspapers have editorial departments which are tough and professional. You must have something exceptional to say to attract them, but many of them do buy from the freelance and specialist knowledge can be welcome. They will also pay for information or even a good idea which their own staff will write. An excellent book on the subject is *Freelance Writing for Newspapers* by Jill Dick, published by A & C Black.

Trade, house and free press
Trade magazines are rarely seen on bookstalls, but they are well worth exploring. Almost every trade or profession has a magazine and some have several. Although there are directories to trade magazines, they are expensive. The easiest way is to ask your local tradesmen or professionals if they get such magazines and, if so, could you see a back copy. The rates of pay from trade magazines vary widely, but some have very high rates.

House magazines are those which are circulated to the employees of large companies. Again, you have to track them down. Some pay well, others not at all. A few will only accept items from their own employees.

There has been a rapid growth in free magazines. Many of them are very professionally produced and some pay among the highest rates in the UK.

The market for articles is undoubtedly vast. Most of these magazines would fold up without freelance contributions. Remember, if you can provide reasonable material, they not only want you, they need you.

Chapter Three

Looking for ideas

A frequent complaint of beginners is, 'I don't know what to write about.' Yet, every writer or would-be writer will know the experience of reading magazine articles and saying ruefully, 'I could have written that.' True, perhaps they could have written it, but they didn't. However, take heart from this for it shows a glimpse of the wide-open range of subjects which are really at your finger-tips. All that these ideas require is the perception and motivation to claim them as your own.

In contrast to the beginner, the established writer invariably has a bulging 'ideas file' and wonders where on earth he can find the time to write it all up. While the beginner sits in front of a blank sheet of paper waiting for inspiration, the more experienced are busy writing, having done much of their thinking in any spare minutes of the day, in the train, driving the car, or even in bed. The latter is particularly valuable for many people because sleeping on an idea can be surprisingly fruitful.

Life is an exciting experience for writers. It is a source of interest and inspiration and a stimulant to curiosity. Perception grows with practice and you will quickly sense the potentials in scraps of conversation, snippets of news and seemingly unexciting experiences.

My wife Molly and I have the good fortune of both being writers. We can toss ideas back and forth, finding that the material which is not suitable for one may be ideal for the other. Quite often, we both use the same material, writing it in our own particular styles and for quite different markets.

There are moments when one of us will say, 'There could be an article in that.' Or, more likely, we just look at each other, tuned in to the same wave-length, knowing that an overheard fragment has revealed interesting potential to us both simultaneously.

Ideas do come with experience. Frequently they are self-generating, for not only will one idea naturally lead to another, but your research often leaves you with far more material than you can use in one article. This can be used for quite different articles or to introduce changes in similar articles for sale to different markets – a perfectly legitimate technique, if done correctly.

'Write what you know about, but . . .'
The usual tip to beginners from old-stagers is, 'Write what you know about!' Sound advice, but certainly not the only way to begin. If you do write about a subject in which you have experience, by all means use it to the full, but try to break out into other fields as soon as you can. It is too easy to become a one-theme writer who has no confidence with other subjects, your speciality becoming a straight-jacket.

You may wonder what experience you have which is worth writing about. Well, there is your job, your hobbies, your human problems or any unique experience. Then look at aspects of the lives of members of your family. Again, human problems are often interesting if sensitively written about – coping with problem children, an elderly and confused parent or an alcoholic. You can always use a pen-name to preserve your anonymity, but such articles can be helpful to others and therapeutic to the writer. If they are success stories against adverse circumstances, particularly if the problems were solved in a unique way, so much the better.

Living with your partner's hobby can be interesting. One of our students wrote an article on living with her husband's photography. She used the 'if you can't beat 'em, join 'em' theme and illustrated it with her own photographs. Another student wrote a poignant personal experience article on the problems of bringing up step-children. Both articles sold.

10

On one of our article-writing courses we had a moving example of the therapeutic power of writing. The student was a young woman who had been suddenly and devastatingly disabled. She could walk only with arm-crutches and was in such constant pain that we had to provide a mattress for her to lie on during lectures. Her concern was how she would manage research. 'How can I get around and interview people? How can I make the contacts to give me ideas?'

What did she know about already? She knew all the trauma of one day being a healthy young woman with a job, a boy-friend, a flat shared with friends and a full social life, and then, following an unexpected operation, being crippled, totally dependent on her parents and cut off from everything. It had taken Margot's last ounce of courage to come on our course.

So, Margot wrote about this experience. She poured out all the hurt and frustration, but also included the realisation that perhaps, after all, there might still be something that life had to offer her. She sold it with no difficulty.

By the end of the week, Margot was writing humour that had us rolling in the aisles.

We had a Christmas card from Margot. 'I am so chuffed with my writing,' she said. 'Have just sold an article to *Annabel* and the editor is asking for more. PS. I'm having another operation soon.'

A month later we had a letter from Margot's mother. 'You will be sad to hear that Margot died two days ago. I felt I had to write to let you know that Margot's writing transformed her life in her last six months.'

I have told Margot's story because the simple truth is, that if Margot with her severe pain and restricted mobility could still generate ideas and write and sell, then so can almost anyone. It all comes down to motivation and the will to succeed.

Three major themes
There is a widely held belief that if all general interest articles were to be broken down into subjects, the majority would fall into three main categories – money, health and

sex. Looking at the three subjects in their broadest interpretation, you may well agree that there could be some truth in it.

Articles on money can include making it and saving it. Making it can cover careers, investment, mortgages, pensions, self-employment, income tax and many other aspects. Saving it could include do-it-yourself jobs, gardening, cheap holidays, wise purchasing and economic motoring, all of which latch onto the 'save' theme.

The do-it-yourself market is worth a special mention. More and more people do their own household repairs, from changing washers to retiling the roof. They build garden sheds, car-ports, garages and even houses. Women have moved competently into these fields and the women's magazines frequently use do-it-yourself articles. Perhaps you have the necessary skills already, so why not pass them on? Perhaps you have found out the hard way. If you made mistakes, it may be better to say so. The article could be practical and helpful or, for a different market, hilarious. How not to do it, perhaps?

Alan Taylor was an amateur do-it-yourself enthusiast. After retirement he began writing articles for do-it-yourself magazines. He found that he had the knack of describing practical work in an easily understood fashion and his articles sold readily. It was a small step to writing do-it-yourself books and these sell world-wide with many of them book club choices. Now in his eighties and still writing, Alan's only complaint is, 'Why didn't I start writing earlier in my life?'

Most of us have our own ideas and techniques when it comes to gardening. There are a great number of gardening magazines which endlessly trot out the same old information. They are itching for something new. Don't imagine that the TV and radio gardening personalities have the corner on this market. I once wrote an original piece for a gardening magazine, only to find it published under the name of one of the gardening celebrities. Fortunately, they paid me, but he would have had his cut as well.

Health is covered by specialist magazines, for both professional and lay readers. Almost every general magazine and particularly women's magazines have their regular slots on health. Articles cover healthy eating and cooking, organic gardening, every slant of physical fitness and, of course, ill-health in all its forms.

Health has endless possibilities which I have used regularly. Some of the themes have been alcoholism, anxiety and depression, the employment of the disabled, drug addiction, stress, the difficulties of caring for the elderly and disabled at home and the problems of living in an institution.

Some people love talking about their operations. Don't talk about them – write about them! Quite a number of magazines publish articles on medical subjects. They can be factual, helpful, reassuring or even funny, but they do sell.

About ten years ago I had an unpleasant ear operation. It entailed chiselling away a piece of my skull and grafting a piece of muscle into the cavity. Before the operation, I looked up neuro-surgery out of curiosity and found it went back to Ancient Egypt and beyond. The day after the operation, Molly found me sitting up in bed, head swathed in bandages, writing the article 'Who needs a hole in the head?' It sold to *She* and a more factual article on the medical aspects sold to *Choice*.

Although I am not medically qualified I have written major articles for numerous medical magazines. These have included the free magazines for doctors, such as *Pulse, Medeconomics, General Practitioner, Current Practice* and others. However, before you try to write for this market I must caution you that it is not easy to break into and requires careful thought and market study. Your GP should be willing to pass on back copies for you to read.

Whether we admit it or not, sex variously intrigues, worries or excites nearly everyone. I remember being the chairman of a lecture by a psychiatrist on 'Counselling sexual problems.' We were staggered at the phenomenal audience – over treble our normal turnout. Incidentally, the lecture provided me with material for an article on the subject for a professional magazine.

Sex could include relationships at all ages, human problems (not necessarily overtly sexual), sex discrimination, women who make good in a man's world and vice-versa. Seen in its widest sense, sex can include personal appearance

– dress, make-up, hair-style and even personality grooming.

Craft magazines take articles on everything from petit-point to sculpture, but they really do need photographs to back them up. Remember, it is not essential for you to have skills in a specific craft if you can write about someone who has.

With our ageing population, occupying oneself in retirement is a major subject. It embraces keep-fit, finances, gardening, special holidays and even sport. Particularly interesting are unusual activities which seem at first sight to be inappropriate for the age group (for example, windsurfing for veterans). There are several specialist magazines in the retirement field.

Holidays can bring a wealth of material. Whether camping, caravanning, back-packing, or even bed and breakfasting, they all offer opportunities. Wander with your car or on public transport, on or off the beaten track, at home or abroad. Talk to local people. Listen to tales of folklore and nostalgia. Roam around castles, churches, graveyards, museums, workshops and unusual industries. Come back home, relive your holiday and write about it. Then sell the articles and help to pay for the holiday. Lastly, and perhaps sweetest of all, agree with your tax inspector whether part of the holiday can be considered a tax expense.

Ideas files

Ideas files are indispensable. They can be in the form of box-files or even books, but they are of the greatest value. Note every scrap of information which catches your imagination and might be useful. If it fascinates you, ask yourself if it would intrigue others. If so, could you gather more supporting information to create an article?

It is of no immediate value to learn a thrilling snippet from Yorkshire if it requires on-the-spot research and you live in London. However, it is worth noting, unless it is very topical, for you could be in that area one day. We keep extensive regional files which yield valuable material when we are going to other areas, but for which special trips would be unprofitable.

Cold news

Many article writers use cold news as a source of material. This can be gleaned from regional TV news and local newspapers, whose reporters ferret out intriguing stories to fill brief slots. These are often one-day wonders, but may well be worth following up after the story has been forgotten.

For example, later in the book I refer to the incident of a serious breach in a canal. When it occurred it received TV and newspaper coverage, but general interest quickly faded. However, several boating magazines were keenly interested in the situation. They needed constant updating on the details of meetings, funding of repairs and prospects for the future. Photographs were required, not only of the breach, but also of signs of dereliction, stranded boats and the ultimate repairs in progress. Not a very high paying market, but a steady one and also a market for future full-length illustrated articles.

Cold news can be valuable, so why not check up to see what did happen to that chap who planned to breed pythons in his garden shed?

More examples

A few more examples from our files may be helpful. A chance reference in a guide book led us to a tiny museum. In the nearby village of Polstead, William Corder had murdered Maria Marten in the notorious Red Barn. As a subject it had been done to death in books, on the stage, on radio and television. Nobody would want an article on 'The Murder in the Red Barn' – or would they?

Our guide-book mentioned some intriguing details so we went along to see. We found a book bound in the tanned skin of the murderer, his scalp, together with one ear, his pistols and other relics of the crime.

My first approach to an editor brought the expected response. 'It's been overdone!' Then I said, 'Wait a minute. I'm not particularly interested in what happened to Maria Marten, but what society did to William Corder. For

15

example, did you know that the Chief Surgeon of the Royal Suffolk Hospital skinned him, tanned the skin and bound a book with it? Also, I have a photograph of the book, his tanned scalp and other relics. How's that for starters?' The result – an instant sale.

I used to be a beekeeper. Molly decided nervously to take it up. Her experiences made alarmingly funny articles. On one occasion we visited a local apiary. The beekeeper had been made redundant from his job and had decided to turn his hobby into a business. Not much of a story there, perhaps, but hold on! How did he go about it?

John Major needed at least 200 hives, but at £100 each the cost was prohibitive. He decided to build his own. He bought the wood straight off the ship at the docks, all £3,000 worth of it, and spent a whole winter making the hives. Then he bred the bees to fill them.

John survived by hard work and ingenuity. He studied bees intensively and discovered new ways of breeding queens. He sold bees, queens and honey. He lectured on beekeeping and ran courses for beekeepers. All the time he sought new and better ways of keeping bees and making equipment. John made a reasonable living in the certain knowledge that, one day, our fickle weather would produce a bonanza year and then he would be knee-deep in honey and a rich man.

It made a fascinating story and sold to several magazines with both black-and-white and colour photographs. *Choice* was running a series of articles on second careers and this was right up their street. The beekeeper had worked for ICI's Fibre Division and they had a house magazine called *Fibres Post*. A quick phone call and they bought an illustrated article on the spot.

Everyone is aware that the use of herbs in cooking and folk medicine is booming. We grow them, use them and Molly writes about them. In researching herbal folklore, Molly came across details of the mandrake. It is a strange plant, believed in Medieval days to have been half-human. It was said to scream when pulled out of the ground and anyone hearing it would die or go mad. People were burned at the stake for possessing it and the whole plant was said to belong to the devil. Research produced a wealth of fascinating legend and old usable prints. We even found an old man who grew them. An article sold to *She* with no problem.

During the mandrake research, we found that the fruit of the plant had been a much sought-after aphrodisiac and a vital ingredient in love-potions. Very little extra research was needed to produce an article on the history of love potions and aphrodisiacs, again snapped up by *She*.

During the same research we came across some hilarious ancient medical folklore. It sold, practically verbatim, to the medical magazine *Pulse*.

Like many people, we have a wild bit in our garden overgrown with stinging nettles. What interest could there possibly be in stinging nettles? Well, the editors of both *She* and *Weekend* obviously thought there was a great deal, for they both bought Molly's articles on the subject which were crammed with fact and folklore.

You would be excused for thinking that there could hardly be a more mundane subject than 'Buttercups and Daisies,' yet an article by Molly on these two ordinary little flowers sold to *The Lady* with no difficulty. She wrote it more or less as a challenge. The same editor bought another one on 'Cobwebs.' How much more down to earth can you get?

One day we were discussing recent tragedies caused by children playing on the shore with air-beds and inflatables. The trouble, we agreed, was that water and boats were fun, but people needed educating about their dangers. The boating press would hardly be interested. We asked ourselves which folk were at greatest risk. The answer was obvious – holidaymakers. Articles slanted to this market were sold to both caravanning and camping magazines. *Practical Caravan* thought the article so valuable that they asked me to re-write it the following year. Re-written yet again and with new colour photographs, it has just sold to another caravanning magazine.

We have an electronic speed controller, or cruise-control, in our car to relieve the strain on long journeys. The device had been well-covered in the motoring press, but we found it a great aid when towing. So articles were sold to both

Practical Boat Owner and *Practical Caravan*. Again, *Practical Caravan* later reprinted it and paid a second fee.

On another occasion, a chance remark in a shop led us to a fantastic character. Geoffrey Ball had volunteered for the RAF in the last war by falsifying his age. He was, in fact, only sixteen at the time. Just after his seventeenth birthday he was flying Spitfires against the Germans. Shot down over France, he was hidden by the Resistance, but was eventually caught by the Gestapo and thrown into the notorious Fresnes prison as a spy. His whole life was an adventure.

After the war Geoffrey eventually took up civilian flying and became a senior captain flying Tri-stars. Unfortunately, when Court Line International collapsed, it took his job, pension and savings with it. Of all things, Geoffrey became a charcoal-burner. He had a home-made kiln, went round as black as soot and built a thriving one-man business. How he achieved this was both enterprising and extremely funny. His story generated a great number of articles and I shall return to it in the chapter on selling your work.

These are brief comments on a small selection of articles, showing how widely varied were the sources of their inspiration. Article material is all around you, but you must learn to be article-conscious, to spot the germ of an idea, to cultivate it in your mind, and if possible to find a new angle on it.

I am well aware that beginners may find this difficult, but once the knack develops it stays and becomes part of your thinking processes, almost as natural and instinctive as breathing.

You will find that, eventually, ideas are born quicker than you can make them into articles and you will become selective, only picking the very best. People often have difficulty in believing they will ever achieve this knack, yet many of them come up to me later and say, 'You were right. I do have more ideas now that I can ever cope with.' If you work at it diligently, it will happen for you too.

Chapter Four

Market research

The corner-stone of successful article-writing is undoubtedly effective market research, making this chapter one of the most important in the book. Its advice is vital for your consistent success, yet far too many would-be writers underestimate the importance of studying the market. In the opinion of all well-established writers, you can only ignore market research at great cost in time and money.

The purpose behind the research is very simple. It is to ensure that your articles suit precisely the markets for which they are intended.

Too often one finds beginners conceiving a gem of an idea and seeing its promise. They write up the article to their own personal satisfaction and then start hunting for someone to buy it. True, one might sell the occasional article this way, but far too many of them will be rejected. As a method, it is about as logical as a dentist making dentures and then looking for a patient they might fit.

Sound and accurate market research is quite a skilled business, but like so many aspects of writing, it quickly becomes second nature with practice.

I am often asked which should come first, the idea or the market. My answer is 'It doesn't matter.' Often it is the idea which comes first, but before you develop it, begin studying possible markets. Reduce these to one or two and then analyse these in fine detail. It is only after this that you can begin tailoring that article to meet the market needs.

Of course, it may start when you see a magazine and recognise its potentials. It may be a new one. Its contents may indicate that you have material which could fit its requirements and again, after fine analysis, you write the article to fit those requirements precisely.

Ready-made market information
There are sources of ready-made market research which are extremely valuable to article-writers. The leader is undoubtedly *The Contributor's Bulletin* from Freelance Press Services, 5/9, Bexley Square, Salford, Manchester, M3 6DB. There are 11 issues a year and the current subscription is £16, post free.

The Contributor's Bulletin, or *CB* as it is known, is packed with information and covers about 60 markets in each issue. It tends to be stronger on articles than fiction.

Another source is the *Market Newsletter* of the Bureau of Freelance Photographers, 497, Green Lanes, London, N13 4BP. There are 12 issues a year and the current cost is £25, but this includes an annual market handbook. Primarily for photographers, it does include some information on article requirements in magazines. The number of markets covered is much less than in *CB*, and the *Newsletter* includes much padding in the form of members' advertisements of photo equipment, readers' letters and editorial comment, the latter often whimsical and having little market relevance. At £25 it is expensive and the handbook, like all market handbooks, must be out-of-date before it reaches the members' hands, with the irritation that you have to have it, whether you want it or not. However, updating of the handbook is given in the *Newsletter*.

Having said that, I subscribe to both and find that they pay for themselves many times over, but I am also a photographer. The *Market Newsletter* sometimes gets 'hotter' news of magazines than *CB*. However, for all article-writers, particularly those who are not photographers, *CB* wins hands down in contents and value for money.

There is also the *Writers' and Artists' Year Book*, published by A & C Black. It is always well out of date by publication, but includes a great deal of information on agents, publishers, copyright, manuscript correction etc., as well as a by no means comprehensive list of magazine markets. For some strange reason, it even includes some markets which don't pay for contributions.

Some magazines, particularly in USA, offer writers' guidelines. Most of these are very valuable, but some can be misleading. For example, the guidelines of one suggested that it was seriously concerned with human problems, but sample copies proved it to be pornographic.

Some give sound, crisp and even entertaining advice. 'Get in there and tell your story, then give us a snappy ending and get out again. Don't try to dazzle us with your footwork!' I liked that one very much.

Some magazines in USA will send free copies, but you must enclose International Reply Coupons (IRC's) which are obtainable from any British Post Office. They are 55p each at present and are only the equivalent cost of surface mail. To get an airmail reply you would be wise to enclose two coupons.

The best source of USA market information is the American book *Writers' Market*. Its cost depends on the rate of exchange, but expect to pay around £20. It is obtainable from Freelance Press Services, mentioned earlier.

Research methods

Doing your own market research means reading magazines in depth. These can be bought, borrowed, begged from friends, read in library reading rooms, dentists' and doctors' waiting rooms and in hairdressers. Never go to such places without a pen and paper.

You can study the markets superficially, by courtesy of Smiths, Menzies and other booksellers. Last year we spent several hundred pounds on magazines solely for research and so we have no qualms at having a browse through the magazine shelves before buying those we need.

Most of the large chain newsagents display their magazines broadly grouped in areas of interest – computers, country-side, caravans, cars, boats, wildlife, women's magazines, for example. This makes it easy to check on new magazines entering a field in which you are interested.

Superficial study is quite inadequate for real market analysis. You need a current issue of the magazine in your hand with time to examine it in depth.

Let us suppose you want to analyse a new magazine in the women's market. Read it through and get the general feel of it. If you still think that it might have potential for your writing interests, start probing more deeply. How frequently is it published, weekly or monthly? What is the price? What is the proportion of fiction to articles? Look at the list of the editorial staff and check how many of them appear as writers of the magazine's articles. Some magazines use a great deal of staff-written material, others rely heavily on freelance contributions. In other words, check what opportunities there are for you.

By studying several issues of a magazine, you can discover the regular freelance contributors. Some of these may be under contract and almost as firmly established as the staff.

In most women's magazines you will find that at least the health, beauty and cooking are written by staff or regulars.

If it is a new magazine, your market research agency (such as the *Contributor's Bulletin*) will almost certainly have mentioned it and may even have obtained the editor's stated requirements. Study the comments. As yet, the rates of pay are probably unknown or may be stated as negotiable, which is a discreet way of saying 'Wait and see!' Its advertising income will be slender and its circulation figures anyone's guess. For established magazines, you can find out the circulation figures of a year or so ago by consulting *Willing's Press Guide*. This is too expensive to buy as a reference book for article-writers, but should be available in your local library.

Try to assess the typical reader of your magazine. The articles will tell you a great deal more than the fiction. For example, don't presume that the heroine in a short story will always be the same age and social class as the reader, for there is a great deal of escapism in magazine fiction.

Many writers tend to skip the advertisements, but these are extremely important. Advertising agencies perform far

22

more sophisticated and professional research exercises than the writer can hope to do. They have to, for ads are the financial life-blood of every magazine. The advertising agencies' own contracts are linked to the reader response to their carefully conceived ads. If they misjudge the typical reader, it could be a very costly mistake for their customer, themselves and ultimately, the magazine. So, as a writer, pick the advertising agencies' brains and benefit from their research.

Looking at the ads can tell you the age group and the social class of the reader more certainly than anything else. It can tell you the type of house she is likely to live in, the car she will drive, the sort of holiday she enjoys, in other words, her income bracket.

There is obvious significance in ads for baby lotion against those for retirement homes, ads for Jaguars against Escorts, hardwood fitted kitchens against self-assembled melamine units.

The articles will require your closest attention. What are they about? How long are they? There is no need to count all the words. Merely count 100 words in a typical column and measure the length they occupy. Then use this as a rough guide against the number of column/inches in the article. You only need an approximation because you are going to find out the exact length requirements later.

Note the style. Is it formal and packed with facts or is it chatty? For example, is there the touch of the lecture about it or does the writer 'talk' to the reader like a close friend? Is the magazine's style fairly rigid or does it vary widely with the subject of the article?

As an example of style, let us suppose that you have just returned from a fabulous package holiday in Darjeeling. You have plenty of photographs and you want to turn your experience into articles. How would you do it?

Market research would dictate your style and for one market you might begin:

Most people would imagine that a holiday in the Himalayas would be out of their reach. I was surprised to

23

find that it can be as easy to arrange as a trip to Jersey and not prohibitively expensive.

Another market might suggest an informal approach, possibly using dialogue, but saying practically the same thing:

It was January and snowing. The central-heating was struggling to cope with the sub-zero temperature and I was day-dreaming of Tenerife.

'How would you fancy a holiday in the Himalayas?' Bill said suddenly.

'You must be joking,' I snapped.

Bill held out a travel brochure. 'No, it's all here.'

The difference is quite obvious. The chatty informal style brings the situation alive, but not all editors would like it that way.

Look at the illustrations. Are they photographs? Colour or black-and-white? Are they artists' impressions or even cartoons? We shall look at illustrations in more detail later.

If I want to break into what I suspect to be a difficult market, I use coloured pens to analyse articles which are similar to my own fields. Each colour has significance for me. For example, for a travel article, I might use green for descriptive passages of scenery, red for details of accommodation, blue for eating out and brown for places of interest, local customs etc.

Although you have tried to establish the type of reader in your mind, you must remember that it is the editor you are selling to, not the reader. The editor, in turn, is making a shrewd guess at what his readers want. In this he is guided by readers' letters, changes in circulation and pats on the back or raps on the knuckles from the publishers. If he is too far out – he goes. (For convenience I am using the masculine pronoun but in fact many editors are women.)

By studying the articles carefully you will see the editor's preferences and how his mind is working. Identify the subjects of the articles. What are they? Try to classify them, using an identification suitable for the specific magazine. In

24

a women's magazine for example, they might be classified under marriage, family, home, leisure, money, work or social problems. You can add headings as necessary.

You don't need to be precise about this – all you are trying to do is to get a good idea of the type of article which the editor favours.

Editors change and here the market research agencies are usually quick to let you know. Look down editorial changes and make a note of any movements affecting the markets for which you write or hope to write.

Editorial requirements also change and sometimes change radically, particularly if sales have been falling. It is obvious that you must keep up to date in your market research, even if you only do this superficially. If I propose to write for a magazine after a lapse of a few months, I always try to get a look at a current issue in the bookshop, checking the editor's name and getting a general 'feel' of the magazine. If there are obvious changes, I buy the magazine and study it more deeply.

When you have written for a magazine successfully, you will know a great deal more about the market and the editor. You will know what he pays or, more precisely, what he pays *you*, for not all contributors get the same. You will know if he gives prompt decisions on whether he wants the article or not. Does he pay on acceptance or publication? Does he pay immediately on publication or is there still a delay? Does he publish promptly or does it sit in his files for months, even years? I recently received a cheque for an article accepted over four years ago and which I had written off in disgust.

It is also important to assess the magazine's future potential for you. If it uses your work regularly and pays well, it is clearly worth holding on to. Another point which I consider is whether the editorial staff are nice to work with. The last thing one wants is all the trouble of battling with editors over a variety of issues.

Recording market information
It is very valuable to keep a record of each market which publishes your work. This could be a card-index or a book

entry. Summarise all the aspects you have assessed in your market study. Note all submissions, with acceptances or rejections. Record speed of response, amount and promptness of payment. Do you get a complimentary copy of the issue in which your article appears?

It is also worth recording on the same entry the titles of similar magazines in the same field. This enables you to assess alternative outlets for an article should the editor of your first market choice be uninterested, and also to select markets for re-writes of the same theme at a later date.

Experience will tell you how much to record. It will be a compromise between how much you would like and how much is essential.

I believe that you only start being professional when you are selective in your markets and are not prepared to let your work go at any price. Once you are established, you must put a value on your work and not drop below that, except for charitable outlets and, perhaps, small magazines for which you have a soft spot.

Do keep an eye open for new magazines, both on the newsagents' shelves and in your market research agencies' bulletins. I have often scored well, getting in on the ground floor by pouncing on the advance notice of a forthcoming launch. I have even managed to get published in a first issue. You, too, could do the same. If you are a subscriber to the market research agencies, you have the edge on all those writers who do not subscribe. This particularly applies to 'hot' information.

Finally, do remember that market research is of limited value unless it is right up to date.

Chapter Five

Researching the material

After reading a factual article, beginners often ask, 'How do you know all these things? How do you manage to remember them?' The answer is that a good writer doesn't need to have the facts in his head or even at his fingertips. His skill is knowing how to lay his hands on them just when he needs them.

It would be easy for me to skip most of this chapter and merely refer the reader to the best book I know on research. It is entitled *Research for Writers* by Ann Hoffman, published by A. & C. Black. I buy every edition as it is updated and find it invaluable.

There are, broadly speaking, two main kinds of facts – those you know and those you can find out.

The facts you know can be drawn from experience or from past research and other gleanings. I know to my cost that nothing is more fickle than my memory and to rely on it as a storage system for detailed facts is ludicrous. I shall go into filing systems later, but it is sufficient to say that these pieces of information must be stored in a logical way so that they can be retrieved with reasonable ease.

Faced with the need to discover facts by basic research, the average beginner is often bewildered.

My first step is often to consult an encyclopaedia, of which I have two sets. The problem with all encyclopaedia is that they are out of date before they are published. Mine are a bit outdated, but nevertheless they do yield valuable basic information, as long as one remembers that knowledge has advanced since they were published. Under many subject headings they also list bibliographies for further reading but, here again, the latest publications will be missing.

Libraries
Your local library is a valuable source of research. To begin with, it is likely to have a modern encyclopaedia, possibly a Britannica.

An excellent guide to information sources is ASLIB, the two-volume directory compiled by the Association for Information Management. It is not in itself a source of material, but rather a signpost to where to get it.

I have to travel to a neighbouring town to see my nearest copy which is well out of date, but still a treasure trove. For example, our last consultation of ASLIB was for a variety of subjects which we both needed. Fruitful ones turned out to be 'stained glass,' 'regional superstitions,' 'pilots' training,' 'occupational health,' plus an address I had been after for weeks. A mixed bag, but what a yield for an hour's work!

It is wise to familiarise yourself with the Dewey Decimal System under which British Public Libraries file their books. This could save you a great deal of time. Enlist the help of the librarian for your special needs. You will often find that they will be extremely helpful, suggesting books, obtaining them for you and, sometimes, even flagging the sections in them which you require.

Remember that the scope of the library service is nationwide and, although it may not be the speediest service, it can eventually obtain the majority of books you are likely to require.

The copyright libraries are fascinating places. They are so-called because every book published in Britain must have a copy lodged at each of these libraries. They are in London, Oxford, Cambridge, Edinburgh and Aberystwyth. All require a reader's ticket for admission and it is wise to write to the library in advance for an application form and conditions. However, it is possible to obtain a day ticket on personal application. It is necessary to have convincing reasons why your research information cannot be obtained elsewhere.

The British Library
The British Library is housed in the British Museum. It was originally called the British Museum Library, and is still affectionately known as the BM to many. It is a vast storehouse of knowledge and information and includes rare and very old books, maps and manuscripts, often unobtainable elsewhere.

As in all copyright libraries, day tickets are available if valid reasons can be provided. A full reader's ticket is more difficult to obtain and your credibility must be established.

Access to books on shelves is very limited at the British Library. The method of obtaining books is to identify the books you require in the catalogue, then fill in the catalogue numbers for these books on application forms, and hand them in at the desk. Unfortunately, you may have to wait several hours before any book arrives. As some books are stored in other parts of London, you may wait all day and still not receive them.

The easiest way round this is to bring away a few application forms with you. Then, when you wish to go to the British Library for research, find out which of your local libraries has a copy of the British Library Catalogue and use that for discovering the catalogue numbers of the books. Fill in the forms and post them to the British Library with several days notice, telling them when you are coming. On your arrival, your books will be waiting for you, although you will still have to wait a short time.

One other piece of advice: when you go to your local library to see the catalogue take a good magnifying glass with you. The catalogue is in miniature with very fine print.

Those of you who specialise must research your speciality in depth. If you are to be considered something of an expert by editors you must not be caught out with inaccuracies. You must keep up to date.

Whatever your method of storing facts, you must note the details of the source of the information. If it is seen on TV or heard on radio, write down the speaker, the programme and the date. Try to write it down straightaway, unless you are recording it for transcription later.

When you come to write the article, keep hold of those notes of your fact sources. I remember Molly writing an article for a magazine which was new to her. The editor wrote back accepting the article, but with one proviso. He said, 'I found some of the facts quite astounding and before proceeding I should be grateful for the sources of your information.'

Molly hadn't noted all of them and it entailed a great deal of work, going back and virtually researching the article all over again.

Other sources
Other sources of information are too numerous to mention specifically and much depends on your subject. Public Relations Officers of industries, government departments and other groups can often be very helpful. Quite frequently they will send out reams of information in response to a specific request.

Tourist boards, both British and foreign, high commissions and embassies are all possible sources of information. I have found the foreign sources very variable. Some have sent me whole books on the subject of my enquiry, others haven't even bothered to reply.

Always try to trace information to its source. There is a great deal of inaccurate material perpetuated by writers who skimp their research and whose writing is then referred to by others. It is a sobering thought to realise that our articles may also be quoted by someone in the future.

Always have more information than you can use in the article on which you are working. Some articles need a great deal of factual material, others need only sufficient to make certain points. It all depends on the nature of the article. If you are thin on facts, it is likely to result in a rather feeble piece.

Some folk tend to look on article-writers as rather lower in the writing hierarchy than, say, novelists, biographers, playwrights and even short story writers. I have heard article-writers described as hacks who collect facts discovered by others, shuffle them like packs of cards and deal each editor a slightly different hand.

I must admit that there is a grain of truth in that opinion. Not that we are hacks, but that we do unearth our facts, shuffle them and deal out a different hand to each editor. However, there should be no element of chance in the way the cards fall. An article-writer will do a great deal of selection and much discarding. There will be considerable reshuffling and a good writer never deals an editor a bad hand.

If you are using facts from personal experience, make sure they are still relevant and valid unless you are writing nostalgia.

As an example of this, I was recently asked by an editor to write a piece on a disused canal which was fast disappearing. How did I go about it?

I checked everything I had on my own records and then went to the library. They obtained all the books on the subject which were readily available, including several which were quite old.

I wrote to the Inland Waterways Public Relations Officer for anything he had and he obligingly sent me some useful material. I knew the canal quite well, but there had been a new road built close to its route. I decided that I must go and see for myself. It was just as well I did for the road had destroyed much of the canal's remains.

It meant that my article was not a mere re-hash of historical facts, although they were included. It was up to date and included personal observations. I was able to say, for example, 'there was something forlorn about this old canal bridge, going nowhere and crossing a mere depression in the ground. Tree roots were already growing in its walls, forcing the stones apart and hastening its destruction.' Backed up by a photograph, it was clear to the reader that I had seen it for myself. Comments like that gave the article an authenticity which would have been missing had I relied on my prior knowledge.

Many writers depend very heavily on interviews for their

material. This aspect of research is dealt with later, but do be aware of the need to check information given to you as facts by interviewees. It could be wrong.

The pitfall of inaccuracies
Including inaccuracies in your article is a certain way of getting an avalanche of readers' letters. The editor doesn't like receiving them and it is a black mark against you. Fortunately I have escaped such attentions from readers in recent years, but I can remember smarting under them in my early days and the criticism was usually well-deserved.

Sometimes interesting and useful material cannot be traced to its source and validated. If it is too good to discard, I use it, but qualify it carefully. For example, one can precede the fact by saying, 'It has been said that . . .' or 'Rumour has it that . . .' or 'The local people believe that . . ..' These are typical ways in which one can use material, without being taken to task for factual inaccuracy. Needless to say, it should not be overdone.

It is only fair to say that some writers look down their noses at this technique, but it is your article and it is up to you how you write it. The ultimate test is that someone buys it.

Falling in love with research
Research can be fascinating. It can even be too fascinating. There are some of us who can actually fall in love with research and forget the real purpose of our quest for information. I know because I have done it.

There are two themes in particular with which I have been hypnotised for years. Both are historical: weaving together the threads of history is notoriously entrancing for its devotees. One has involved me in countless hours of study at the British Library. It has led to correspondence with people at the far corners of the earth. I have travelled on foot in rugged hill districts, carrying heavy cameras and equipment. However good the resulting photographs, they have never been good enough to satisfy me completely. Believe it or not, after years of work I have yet to write an article on the subject.

The other piece has needed no less research, more travelling and even roughing it on an uninhabited island. I have used aspects of my island trip in articles, but the main theme has never been written, despite the passage of the years.

Irrational though it may be, the subject is too profound for the research ever to be completed and the material has become too precious to waste on a mere article. So learn from my mistakes. Don't let research take over and dominate you. Your aim is to write, not to become a researching lotus-eater. Having said that, I enjoyed every minute of the research and I know I would do it all again.

Chapter Six

Interviewing

Sound interviewing can be the backbone of many articles and can breathe life into otherwise dry factual pieces. Yet, some writers feel so uneasy about interviewing that they will go to any lengths to avoid it. If a writer finds such face to face encounters really stressful, then the tension will be transmitted to the subject and the interview is likely to be a very poor one. In these circumstances, it would probably be wise for such writers to avoid interviewing altogether. Although interviews can be extremely valuable, they are by no means essential for article-writing.

Such stress is not to be confused with the normal nervousness which a novice usually experiences when facing an interview or the apprehension of preparing for 'the big one.' These feelings are natural and diminish with practice. To side-step interviewing because of a passing flutter in the stomach would be to miss out on many memorable experiences, to forego enjoyable conversations with fascinating people, to say nothing of sacrificing a wealth of material and first-class articles.

I recommend that, unless you are a very introverted and anxious person, you should be prepared to take on interviews, choosing your first subjects carefully and making appropriate preparations. Developing your skills will give you confidence, until interviewing becomes a pleasurable aspect of your writing.

Interviewing can take many forms. At its simplest, it may be no more than a straightforward chat. The purpose may be to glean a little information which may have only a minor place in the finished article.

34

Pressure interviews

At the other extreme is the 'pressure' interview, beloved of selection boards and often used in journalism to wring information out of the reluctant interviewee.

Pressure techniques are often used on radio and TV in political interviews. Make no mistake about it, in these circumstances not only is the interviewer highly trained in the interviewing skills, the other party is likely to be well trained also.

Some writers say, 'I'm not tough enough for this sort of interview. I couldn't demand answers and make people feel uncomfortable.' If it is any consolation, neither could I. I have no stomach for dragging information out of reluctant subjects, information which they would probably regret giving the moment they had done so. For me, writing must be a pleasure. If I ever went away from an interview feeling that I had left someone unhappy, someone who would look back on the encounter as an unpleasant experience, then my writing would cease to give me that pleasure.

Many years ago I was trained in pressure interviewing techniques, but I have never used them for journalism. This is where the freelance scores. He is never *told* by an editor to interview someone. If asked to do so, he can always decline if the job is likely to be distasteful or against his personal code of ethics. In practice, the position rarely arises.

Top-flight interviewers are intensively trained and may have years of experience, but the skills necessary for a freelance article-writer are quite modest. However, with experience, these skills develop and writers get an intuitive feel for the right questions to ask and for the areas rich in material. Hopefully, they also gain a sensitivity which tells them when to back off.

There are basic guidelines, a few rules and numerous tips which can help a novice make their early efforts less painful and more fruitful.

Tape-recording and note-taking

One of the most common questions I am asked is, 'Should I take notes or should I use a tape-recorder?' It really depends on the interview and your own feelings about their use. If I am looking for no more than a few basic facts, then I take notes. Here, a spiral-backed shorthand notebook is ideal. It is a handy size and folds flat. I can't write shorthand. I wish I could. I use longhand with abbreviations of my own. If taking notes, always carry at least two spare pens.

For the interviewee's benefit, I pass off my note-taking by saying casually that I take notes to ensure I make no mistakes due to lapse of memory. I have never had anyone question my note-taking or appear uneasy about it.

Try to maintain eye-contact with your subject for as much of the time as possible and don't keep your face buried in the notebook. With practice, it is surprising how much you can write without actually looking at what you are doing.

Never hesitate to ask for difficult names to be spelt. Always question inconsistencies or facts which seem illogical.

Obviously, you won't try to write everything down verbatim. You will quickly learn to write down the key points, retaining the details in your head. On leaving the interview, expand those notes as soon as possible. I drive round the corner, stop the car and write up everything I need. The memory can be fickle and you never know what situation might occur to push things out of your mind.

The use of a tape-recorder has points for and against. Always ask if a tape-recorder is acceptable. Never take it for granted. Some people will refuse to allow it. Others are clearly uneasy, but forget all about it in a few minutes.

Tape-recorders give full details of the interview which you can play back and analyse at leisure. But you can get to rely on them and they can have a nasty trick of letting you down. Batteries go flat, tapes run out unnoticed, volume settings can be too high or too low, or the machine can go faulty and either stop or chew up yards of tape.

Personally, I like a tape-recorder. However, I am a 'belt and braces' man and I still take notes of the salient points of the interview, giving me something to fall back on. I check the tape on leaving the interview, in case I have to expand those notes immediately.

I use one of the miniature models. They are lightweight

and unobtrusive, but the tapes for mine only run for 30 minutes each side. In most cases this means changing over the tape during the interview, a practice which I admit is a distraction. A stop-watch is very useful here. Some of the digital watches with a stop-watch facility can be obtained for a pound or two. Place it by the tape-recorder and break off the interview at a convenient place a few minutes before the tape runs out. I don't pretend this is infallible, for time flies in a fascinating interview. Find the optimum volume setting for recording at, say, four feet distance and mark the volume control accordingly. Be prepared to modify the setting if the distance is different or the speaker's voice varies from the average. I prefer to test the recorder before I reach the interview. Finally, always check the batteries before you go. I use re-chargeable cells and I can ensure they are fully charged each time. I still take spare batteries and also a spare tape or two.

That first interview
Armed with the tools of your trade, how do you start out on the interview business? I advise you to avoid well-known personalities. Usually, they have been through it all countless times with skilled interviewers and are well practised in the cut and thrust of such encounters. They may be very understanding, telling you everything you want to know (or they want you to know) without your asking a question. They may be irritated by your inexperience and show it. There may even be those who get some pleasure from your discomfort.

Whatever their attitude, it is unlikely that you will come away with anything new and your proposed article will excite few editors. I don't say that you will have learned nothing, but you will have had no opportunity to practise that vital skill of putting your subject at ease.

Among the best interviews for the tiro to cut his teeth on are those of an unknown individual whose unique story is likely to intrigue readers.

Ground work

Having found such a character, you should try to uncover as much as you can about them before the interview. If they specialise in some skill or have an unusual hobby, for example, then you should research this in advance also.

When I first heard of Geoffrey Ball, the pilot turned charcoal-burner, the tale sounded so bizarre that I took much of it with a pinch of salt. However, I looked up charcoal-burning in my encyclopaedia for the basic facts. I then phoned, saying I was freelance journalist, asking if he would be agreeable to an interview. His wife, Diana, invited me along without hesitation.

My friendly librarian had found as much reading material on charcoal-burning as she could and I felt reasonably well briefed for the interview. Prior research means that you can ask pertinent questions and can absorb the answers more intelligently. In any case, I am sure Geoffrey felt I was paying him a compliment by clearly having taken the trouble to prepare myself in advance.

As I have already said, the truth proved to be more fascinating than the hearsay and the outcome was one of my most memorable interviews.

The beginning

So, you find yourself face to face with your first subject, what should you do to get the most out of the interview? The chances are that, if your subject is an unknown, they will be no less nervous than you are. I would advise against saying, 'This is my first interview,' or 'I am new to this.' You are the initiator of this interview and you must try to remain firmly in the driving seat. Your confidence reassures the nervous subject.

Of course, no two interviewers have the same approach, ask the same questions or end up with the same information. Some might push hard and achieve little; others might have what appears to be a superficial chat and yet drain the subject dry of information. The fact is that certain interviewers do best with certain subjects.

Initially, you could talk lightly about the reason for your

coming and, perhaps, the magazine for which the article is intended. After the ice is broken, check that a tape-recorder is acceptable. Don't switch it on until the interview proper begins – it wastes tape.

On your notebook you should have written a list of material you want to get from your subject. You will have compiled this from your prior information and research. Somehow you must try to get all this material before you leave the interview, irrespective of other fascinating things which may be discussed. Too many times in the early days, I came away from an interview kicking myself for failing to ask an important question.

The advice often given to beginners is never to ask questions which can be answered with a mere 'yes' or 'no.' It is true that open-ended questions provide richer responses. However, don't be afraid of yes/no questions for they have their place.

Always begin with soft, easy questions, requiring the sort of answer which you feel the subject will enjoy giving. From these you can progress to more probing questions.

Once I have most of the material facts, I often like to talk about feelings. 'How did it feel to . . .?' or 'What was your reaction to . . .?' I like to see my subject pause and think, then I know that memories are being invoked and moments relived. I am less happy about the snap answer to such questions.

I always end as I began, on an easy relaxed note.

Problem interviews and how to tackle them
What problems are you likely to come across? Sooner or later there will be the inevitable difficult customer. Keep cool. Be polite. Gather as much as you can, remembering that you are a freelance and, if you wished, you could walk out of the door and drop your notes in the nearest refuse bin. However, many an excellent article has emerged from a tough and unpromising interview.

You will get the subject who wants to tell the story in his way. You may have the feeling that he has recounted the story with relish so many times that he is word perfect.

39

Sometimes, letting him finish and then going back with your pertinent question is easier than battling with him every inch of the way. It may also get him in a good mood.

Sometimes subjects just take over the interview and chatter away about anything but the subject which should be under discussion. This takes polite firmness to control. One trick is to wait until they are drawing a breath and then jump in with a bold or even startling question which commands attention.

A not uncommon phenomenon is the spouse who wants to take over, answering all the questions while the subject remains silent. I have even known a wife send her husband to make us tea while she continued with *his* interview. The only answer is to be patient, but firm. Try saying something like, 'You're doing all the work and letting your husband get away with saying nothing, Mrs Bloggs. I must persuade him to talk to me or my editor will be cross.' or 'I'm afraid I have to leave shortly and there are still some important questions that I must ask Mr Bloggs. Without them I shall be unable to write the article and that would be a pity.'

Many subjects find it fascinating to be talking to a real writer and say so. They are agog to know about *you*. How did you start? What have you written? What are you doing next? It may be a temptation to relax and respond in order to keep the interview informal and friendly. Keep a tight rein on such inclinations. You don't want to run out of tape or, at best, have to listen to a long recording of one of your own ego-trips.

Beginners often find silences very disturbing. Don't be put off by silences. Sometimes the subject is thinking; sometimes he may be wondering whether or not to disclose something. Watch for body language – facial signs, fingers, hands, feet, posture. If you feel the subject is getting really uneasy or agitated, then break the silence.

As the subject warms to you, he may say something which he later regrets. 'I wouldn't like you to mention what I just said about my father.' Reassure him immediately. If you had written it down, score it out and let the subject see you do so. If it was taped, say, 'I'll make a note that it isn't to be used' and do just that.

Some people ask if they can read and approve the article before it goes for publication. They may even make it a condition of giving the interview. I find that writers are divided in their opinions about this. My own attitude is quite clear. *You* are writing this article, not the interviewee. If they start insisting on changes, you could end up with a diluted, emasculated piece of writing, not in your style, which could prove to be unsaleable.

Make it quite clear that if, on reflection, they wish to have anything which has been said in the interview excluded from the article, you are quite agreeable. I believe you should not go beyond that, and if necessary, you should consider refusing the interview. There are plenty more fish in the sea. Having said that, I must admit that there are just one or two people from whom I might be prepared to accept those terms and, in the end, the decision must be yours.

If, when writing your article, you find there is a point which is unclear, don't be afraid to ring up and ask for clarification. Try to go right through the article first and check if there are any other points. This avoids repeated phone calls which might be irritating.

I always write and thank the subject for the interview. Finally, it is courteous to send them a copy of the magazine in which the article appears.

Beginners still press me for typical questions to use in interviews. They ask for specific questions I have used. I often give as an illustration the following – an interview which never actually took place, and I ask for suggestions of suitable questions.

We were tutoring a residential course on creative writing. On a parallel course was a charming little old lady who, we were told discreetly, had enjoyed an unusual career. She had been a human cannon-ball. The implication was that she was self-conscious about this and we sadly abandoned any idea of a story. It was only some years later that we found out to our dismay that she would have been delighted to have talked to us. It was an occasion when sensitivity didn't pay off.

Since then we have posed the question to our students, 'Had that interview taken place, what sort of questions should we have asked?'

Most people agree that an important question would be, 'Why did you become a human cannon-ball?' Perhaps circuses fascinated her, or she wanted to get away from home, or she fell in love with the lion-tamer.

Then there are the technicalities. 'How are you fired from a cannon?' 'What are the dangers?' 'How were you trained?'

You could ask about anything unusual, such as amusing or embarrassing moments.

I said I liked to talk about feelings. An obvious question would be, 'Tell me about your feelings the first time you were ever fired out of a cannon.' Followed by, 'How about the first time before an audience?' One could even ask, 'What were your feelings on the last occasion you performed your act?' Finally, 'What are your strongest memories about your act?'

This is not a definitive list, but a few suggestions of typical questions which, quite clearly, would have produced a great deal of material leading to further avenues for discussion.

I have covered the subject of interviewing at some length. I consider it to be important. People are important; they are fascinating and their activities are endlessly various. From our point of view, a salient feature is that their stories can be eminently saleable.

Finally, I repeat that it is wise to be cautious about information given by interviewees as factual. Check if possible or offer it as their opinion only.

Chapter Seven

Building the article

The greatest hurdle for most beginners is getting those first few words down on paper.

Procrastination is the curse of a good many writers. Some call it writers' block, some admit to sheer laziness, others have confessed that they lack confidence and are afraid of failing. Whatever the cause, most of us can find plausible excuses for not getting down to writing until a more auspicious time and too many of us are easily side-tracked.

We are not prima donnas, we are writers. I don't believe in waiting for inspiration. The only answer to procrastination is self-discipline. I pin my faith on setting a time for working and then adhering to it.

Try to set a time when there will be few interruptions. Insist on starting right on time, no matter what happens. Keep writing doggedly, even though the words may not flow and it all seems nonsense.

I find that I need some time to 'tune-in' to my subject and this makes short bursts of writing relatively much less productive than spells of at least two hours. Others can scribble away in any odd moment, but I believe that most of us do our best work when we have time for this tuning-in process.

Writers' block

I recognise that, for some people, 'writers' block' does exist. There are, for example, times when crises blot out all else. Few would write at their best, waiting for the bailiffs to

43

arrive – yet, strangely, some would. The sheer therapy of 'writing out' their anguish can push some writers to great achievements.

We all have times when we write better than others. Discover your prime writing time. I am an early morning bird myself. Write when at your best, but gradually push the threshold out until you can write well for most of the time.

The best book I know on harnessing your emotions for writing is that superb evergreen *Becoming a writer* by Dorothea Brande, MacMillan Papermac. Published over 50 years ago, it is just as valuable today. But don't skim it – read it!

She stresses that writers have two sides – roughly, the emotional and the practical. These, she says, must be balanced for effective creative work. Firstly, they should be taken apart, examined and understood. Then they should be trained, before being married together into a balanced harmonious whole. She gives exercises for doing this.

Dorothea Brande suggests that writers having difficulty should get up a half-hour or more earlier than usual. They must not speak to anyone, turn on the radio or TV, look at newspapers or open the post. They should sit down and *write*. Write anything which makes some sort of sense. The aim is to build a habit of writing during that creative state between sleeping and being awake.

You must read her book for the full exercises. John Braine followed her advice and said it worked wonders for him. I certainly recommend it.

If I need to marshal my resources to work through a difficult piece, I use deep-relaxation and Molly does the same. There are books and tapes which can help in this field, but a really good teacher is invaluable. I lie on the floor and relax progressively. Then I focus my mind on the material in hand. It works wonderfully for me.

The main point is to tackle your 'block' in some way. Don't accept it and give in. For most people, writing your way through it is probably the easiest way.

Some articles seem to progress logically. The do-it-yourself article is a good example, whether you are writing about building a cupboard or cooking a chicken. The opening will be relatively easy to write, followed by the step-by-step instructions from beginning to end. All quite straight-forward and posing no problems.

The articles that cause trouble are those which have no obvious beginning or end. They are, perhaps, packed with facts of more or less equal importance. Even more testing are the so-called 'think-pieces,' those collections of quotations, ideas, opinions and personal experiences, all richly larded with facts.

Beginners often look in bewilderment at the mass of material they have gathered and ask, 'How on earth do I begin?' Obviously some system for sorting and evaluating the material is necessary – a method of correlating information which enables the writer to get a broad idea of the article's final shape. All writers have their own tricks and gimmicks to discipline their minds, but non-linear flow-of-thought patterns are by far the best I have yet found.

Non-linear thought patterns

Molly adopted non-linear note-taking many years ago. I saw the strange sprawls on her notebooks and dismissed them as another of her endearing eccentricities. I was wrong. Once I had appreciated the principle behind it, I realised that here was a technique which would be of immense value for writers. We now use them for note-taking, market research, interviewing, but most important of all, for building articles.

Since adopting them some years ago, I have discovered they are being used by professionals in many fields, particularly in preparing for high-power interviewing.

The principle is quite simple and very logical. We are not, by instinct, linear thinkers, yet we all tend to see everything in a linear fashion, partly due to our training and from the way we read. In other words, our thoughts on a subject tend to be seen in our mind's eye like a shopping-list, one after another. As we think our way down the list, each new item tends to restrict further thinking on those preceding. However, non-linear thought patterns radiate out from a central point.

Supposing, for example, I were building a simple article on, say, my pet subject of bats, but presuming I knew relatively little about them. By linear thinking I could write a list of the little I did know.

Like most people, my impressions of bats would probably be drawn from folklore and too many Dracula films. I might realise that they were the only mammals capable of true flight. I may have heard that their survival is threatened. I may know they hibernate in winter. I may also know they use some sort of echo-location for finding their way in the dark. All this I could write down with question marks against uncertainties. It would look something like this:

BATS.
Only flying mammals?
Hibernate
Threatened species
Echo-location
Blind
Fears
Get in your hair
Vampires
Dracula
etc

With creative thought patterns, the non-linear and natural function of our thought processes are free to use their full power.

I would write the word 'Bats' in the centre of a large sheet of paper. Then I would draw radiating lines leading to the facts in our list and adding further spurs with any conclusions or queries, as in the diagram. This would give me a simple framework on which I could continue building. Research would yield more factual material and would allow me to validate or reject my assumptions.

I would go on building my material in a radiating pattern until I had all my known facts laid out before me. I can add to it as I wish. I can link appropriate points which are associated, using lines, shading, translucent highlight pens or circling items with coloured ink.

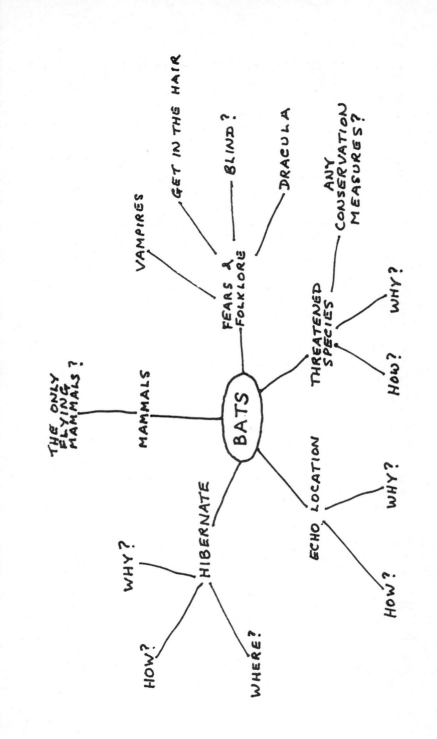

BATS

MAMMALS — THE ONLY FLYING MAMMALS?

FEARS & FOLKLORE
- VAMPIRES
- GET IN THE HAIR
- BLIND?
- DRACULA

THREATENED SPECIES
- ANY CONSERVATION MEASURES?
- WHY?
- HOW?

HIBERNATE
- WHY?
- HOW?
- WHERE?

ECHO LOCATION
- WHY?
- HOW?

You will be surprised how thoughts are triggered by these patterns – new concepts, new slants, new associations of ideas.

If one aspect proves to be particularly rich in material, you may decide to extract it from the main pattern and develop a thought pattern of its own.

Using these patterns enables you to drain the maximum from your knowledge as well as your research. It ensures that you are in a position to marshall this material for use to the best possible advantage.

A typical progression on the general subject of bats, but narrowed for simplicity to 'British bats' is shown in this diagram. This is by no means comprehensive and, in any case, would be used selectively. You will see that major aspects of the subject are easily identified. Sub-themes, rich enough in material for individual development, stand out clearly.

Sketching thought patterns are unnecessary for many articles, but they are a very valuable tool for beginners and also for the established writer when writing a complex article or when things are just not going right. I still use them very often and find them extremely helpful. For further reading on non-linear thought-patterns read *Use your head* by Tony Buzan, BBC Publications. Although the methods shown in this book differ slightly from ours, the principles are the same.

When your article is completed, file the pattern away for use when writing on the same subject in the future.

Before sketching my patterns, I ask myself three questions. Is there sufficient material here for more than one article? If so, which article should I write first and for which market? What slant shall I give the selected article?

We can look at each question in turn. Firstly, is the material sufficient for one article or more than one? Study it carefully, but don't be tempted to stretch the material to make three weak articles instead of being contented with one strong one.

If there is considerable material, decide whether the subject is to be handled in a general sense, a narrow one or possibly both.

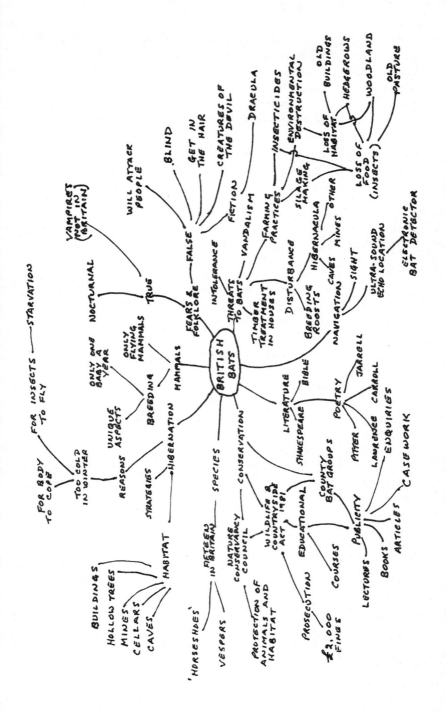

BRITISH BATS

FEARS & FOLKLORE
- INTOLERANCE
- FALSE
  - WILL ATTACK PEOPLE
  - BLIND
  - GET IN THE HAIR
  - CREATURES OF THE DEVIL
  - DRACULA
  - FICTION
- TRUE
  - NOCTURNAL
  - VAMPIRES (NOT IN BRITAIN)

MAMMALS
- ONLY ONE BABY A YEAR
- ONLY FLYING MAMMALS
- BREEDING
- HIBERNATION
  - REASONS
    - UNIQUE ASPECTS
    - TOO COLD IN WINTER
    - FOR BODY TO COPE
    - FOR INSECTS TO FLY → STARVATION
  - STRATEGIES
- HABITAT
  - BUILDINGS
  - HOLLOW TREES
  - MINES
  - CELLARS
  - CAVES

THREATS TO BATS
- VANDALISM
- FARMING PRACTICES
  - SILAGE MAKING
  - INSECTICIDES
- ENVIRONMENTAL DESTRUCTION
  - LOSS OF HABITAT
    - OLD BUILDINGS
    - HEDGEROWS
    - WOODLAND
    - OLD PASTURE
  - LOSS OF FOOD (INSECTS)
- TIMBER TREATMENT IN HOUSES
- DISTURBANCE
  - HIBERNACULA
    - CAVES
    - MINES
    - OTHER
  - BREEDING ROOSTS
- NAVIGATION
  - SIGHT
  - ULTRA-SOUND ECHO LOCATION
    - ELECTRONIC BAT DETECTOR

CONSERVATION
- SPECIES
  - 15 TAXA IN BRITAIN
  - 'HORSESHOES'
  - VESPERS
- NATURE CONSERVANCY COUNCIL
  - PROTECTION OF ANIMALS AND HABITAT
  - WILDLIFE & COUNTRYSIDE ACT 1981
    - PROSECUTION
    - £2,000 FINES
  - EDUCATIONAL
    - COURSES
  - COUNTY BAT GROUPS
  - PUBLICITY
    - LECTURES
    - BOOKS
    - ARTICLES
    - CASEWORK
    - ENQUIRIES

LITERATURE
- BIBLE
- SHAKESPEARE
- POETRY
  - JARRELL
  - PITTER
  - LAWRENCE CARROLL

As an example of this, Molly had been researching the subject of ferns, their structure, propagation, folklore etc. She decided it would make a nice general interest article and sold it to *She*. Narrowing it down from the general to the specific, she wrote another article on bracken, sifting out the facts relating to this species. This sold to *Gamekeeper & Countryside*. Her marketing decisions clearly influenced her selection and use of the material.

Finding a slant

Is the article to be given a particular slant? In other words will it be given a special perspective to make it more interesting or, perhaps, to meet the needs of a specific readership? For example, the bracken article could have been slanted to farmers, stressing bracken as an agricultural problem, probably drawing on Ministry information about its control or eradication. It is worth bearing in mind that such a readership often likes a little general information, even folklore, to brighten up the piece.

The ferns article could have been written for a gardening magazine, slanted to give advice on cultivation, propagation, pests and diseases, plus a list of varieties and, again, a little folklore.

Clearly, the intended slant is an important factor in your concept of the completed article and it must be firmly in your mind before you begin your draft.

So, we have our subject, possibly narrowed to a single aspect and perhaps slanted to a readership viewpoint. Where do we go now?

I use my flow-of-thoughts pattern now. Quite often a few minutes' consideration will be sufficient to crystallise the outline in my mind and I can begin writing. If, however, it is a difficult subject or a tough market, I would take a great deal more time over it. I advise beginners to tackle all articles in the following way until they gain experience.

I sketch my thought patterns in some detail, continuing to expand points and delete irrelevancies as I go along. If it gets too cluttered, I redraw it. Finally, I have all the key points of my research, my thoughts, my experiences and quotations clearly before me. It is from this pattern that I decide the relative importance of the various elements and sub-themes. Which ones shall I stress? Which shall I merely cover superficially? Which ones shall I link together and how shall I do it? Which is the best order for the many points I wish to cover? How shall I start the article? How shall I finish?

I am now ready for drafting the basic framework of the article, after which I shall start putting flesh on the skeleton with words.

The opening
For most articles, the opening paragraph is vitally important. A good opening will hold the editor's attention and make him read on. He will instinctively know that it should have the same effect on the reader of the magazine. Conversely, a poor opening read by a busy editor may precipitate a rejection slip, despite the fact that the overall article may have merit.

I write my opening paragraph in the full realisation that I shall probably re-write it when the article is completed. Sometimes, my first attempt at the opening satisfies me and I leave it, but more often than not it is altered radically.

How do you make your opening grab the editor? Look at your thought patterns and see if any point is intriguing, eye-catching, controversial or even sensational. If it is, check to see if it could be used in the opening without altering your proposed balance of the article. For example, a fact might be intriguing, but it might also need a lengthy preamble before its meaning could be grasped by the reader. This might make it too long and lacking in impact for an opening paragraph. If it appears practical, use it in a punchy opening which makes the reader want to read more.

In my article on the mandrake for *She*, I opened with:

If ever a plant could be said to be dedicated to the devil, it must be the mandrake. Make no mistake, *Mandragora officinarum* is a dangerous plant, narcotic and poisonous. Carefully measured doses were used by the ancients in love philtres and aphrodisiacs, but there were many miscalculations which brought madness or death. The Emperor Julian spoke of Calixenes drinking mandrake juice nightly as a love-stimulant, but Shakespeare called it "the insane root which takes the reason prisoner!"

An opening for *En Route,* the caravanning magazine, was intended to intrigue.

The variety of pets taken on holiday in caravans is truly astonishing, but our contribution is declared by most people to be the strangest of them all. We have no option but to take our pets with us, for who on earth could you ask to look after your contingent of bats?

Giroscope, the magazine for National Girobank customers, was a good market until its size was reduced. However, it needed some financial 'hook' to interest its editor. I was commissioned to write an article on caravanning for him. Under the title, 'Feel Free!' I began: .

These days of increasing holiday costs have made bargain-hunting a priority, with self-catering enjoying a boom. Whether it is a question of holiday economics or the unsuspected gypsy in our souls, more people are turning to caravanning, which is "come and go as you please" self-catering par excellence.

My second paragraph reinforced the economy theme and stated that caravans can quickly pay for themselves.

Sometimes I use quoted speech as an opening. For example, in an article on the problems of being physically disabled I used the words of a disabled girl, Julie.

If only I could storm out and slam the door behind me sometimes. But just you try doing that effectively in a wheelchair.

Her words did, I hope, encapsulate a little of the stress and frustration of being disabled, bringing it home to the reader.

Readers' Digest tends to go in for punchy openings and is well worth studying to note how they get their effect.

The body

We now come to the body of the article which will focus on the main theme. Some beginners work hard on their opening paragraph and then believe they can get away with the bulk of their article consisting of no more than a whole catalogue of facts. Others may offer as the body of their article a boring uninspired ramble through a sparse sprinkling of facts.

The opening should be a hook, forcing the reader to carry on, but the best opening paragraph will never hold a reader through the tedium of a boring article.

You should have earmarked the points in your thought pattern which are logically associated, either by using translucent ink or circling them with a selection of coloured pens. Bring these points together to form basic draft passages for your article. Doing this helps to prevent 'grass-hoppering,' that irritating practice where the article jumps back to a previous point as an apparent after-thought.

These passages can now be considered in relation to each other. You will find that some may be improved by integration, others should be discarded altogether. Shift them about until their sequence appears logical.

The ending

At this stage it is probably wise provisionally to earmark the way you wish to end the article. Rarely should this be a mere 'recap' of the main points made in the article. Its form depends largely on the type of article and your approach to it. It may be in the form of conclusions drawn from your arguments. I can only say, perhaps rather enigmatically, that the ending should be 'satisfying.'

It might be helpful to look at the endings of the articles of which I quoted the openings.

In the mandrake article, I went on to describe how the plant was believed to have been half-human and anyone digging it up, without certain elaborate rituals, would die or go mad. My last paragraph was:

> The mandrake, coveted yet feared for thousands of years, has an evil history which sets it apart from all other living plants. Its half-human attributes may be pure superstition, but if you found one growing, could you pull it up without feeling even a small shiver of apprehension?

The 'caravanning bats' article was conservation-oriented and it ended simply with the details of where further information on bats could be obtained.

Bearing in mind the commercial nature of *Giroscope*, it was appropriate to end on a financial note:

> If you are thinking of buying a caravan, remember that very large discounts on new ones can be obtained for cash. For instance, I bought a new caravan last year and, by shopping around, I was able to get a reduction of 15%. A National Giro Personal Loan, of course, allows you to pay cash and you can apply for such a loan to buy a caravan.

I am sure the editor found the crafty last sentence irresistible. In addition I added a few useful addresses.

Now, as you start giving the article the words which will establish its quality as a piece of writing, you must begin looking at it as a whole. The words you use will set the style, pace, balance and general readability.

All along you should have kept the nature of your market in mind, but it now becomes extremely important.

Your ability to turn your basic material into an attractive, well-balanced and, of course, saleable piece of writing will rest on those personal skills which largely come from reading, from a love of words and from practising your craft of writing as often as possible.

Using dialogue
I like to introduce dialogue or quoted speech where it seems

appropriate. If done well, it appears to breathe life into an otherwise rather flat article.

Obviously, you are unable to use interviews verbatim. They would be too long and boring. You may feel reluctant to alter the spoken words of the interviewee, but rest assured this is perfectly acceptable. You write the true sense rather than the spoken word, cutting irrelevancies, pruning non-essentials and leaving the 'meat.' In conveying the sense in quoted speech, it is important to use words and expressions which would be appropriate for the speaker.

Always keep note of any particularly apt or telling phrases. I told you of Julie's words which I used. On a similar theme, a disabled young man in a wheelchair said, 'A two inch step is my Mount Everest!' I used it in a medical article.

Talking to a fellow beekeeper of John Major's, I picked up the opinion, 'John Major? After 30 years that man thinks like a bee.' I used that too.

In writing dialogue, don't be afraid of using 'said.' So many beginners, particularly when writing fiction, feel that they should avoid it at all costs. Instead of 'he said,' we find they use 'he groaned, grated, hissed, snapped, snarled . . .' and a host of other contrived verbs.

Even 'said' can often be left out. For example, 'Geoffrey Ball drew on his pipe, "You know, I never believed I would end up a charcoal-burner." '

Structure

Broadly speaking, articles tend to be a compact form of writing, economical of words and taut in style. After all, they often have a great deal to say in short space. However, there are obvious exceptions to this and some published articles are even long-winded.

The compact format encourages shorter sentences and shorter paragraphs. Indeed, the narrow width of the average magazine column would make a long paragraph appear a solid and unattractive block of print. If you read your work aloud you will detect any lack of smoothness in its construction. A series of short, clipped, staccato sentences may have their place in certain circumstances. They may be used for emphasis or heightening dramatic effect.

The account of a first solo hang-glider flight, for example.

'OK? You're on your own!'
I ran down the hill. Stomach a knot of panic. White knuckles aching with tension. The wind whistled. The harness tightened. Wind noise rose ominously. The ground fell away. Too late to stop. My God, I'm flying!

However, used inappropriately, such short sentences could introduce discord.

Paragraphs generally contain only one subject or concept, but an overlong paragraph can be split up for convenience. You should always try to achieve a smooth transition from one concept to another.

Grammar

Fowler's Modern English Usage, Oxford University Press, is a good reference book on grammar, punctuation and on words which are commonly misused. An excellent book on the correct use of words is *The right word at the right time*, Readers Digest. You will find it invaluable.

Articles rarely aim at literary perfection. Grammar should be sound, but not pedantic. Many old rules are now regularly broken. For example, the beginning of sentences with conjunctions, such as 'and' or 'but,' is a common practice. I must admit that it can be used to good effect and I use it sparingly myself.

Beginners frequently introduce too many adjectives and adverbs. Go over your writing carefully and check to see if each adjective and adverb is doing a vital job in its sentence. If not, cut it out and look for a stronger verb to convey the sense you are looking for.

Watch out for split infinitives. Some are obviously wrong, others can sneak in unnoticed. The famous Star Trek example 'To boldly go where no man has gone before' has been repeated thousands of times worldwide and, frankly, seems to sound more impressive than the correction.

Your use of elision, 'didn't' instead of 'did not,' for example, depends on the market, the type of article and lastly on your own preference. The simplest test is to ask, 'In its context, does it sound right?' It is, of course, perfectly acceptable in quoted speech. Sometimes you will find that using 'did not' will suitably strengthen the sentence. For this reason, it isn't essentially incorrect to use both styles in the same piece.

Pruning, shaping, and polishing
When the first draft of the article is completed, start pruning and shaping. As it approaches the required length, read it aloud, using the punctuation as it is written, not as you think it should sound. Check for euphony, editing those words and phrases which may be technically correct, but sound wrong in juxtaposition.

Take another look at the first paragraph and alter or rewrite it, if necessary.

Finally reduce to the correct length and then hone and polish until you feel that it is the best of which you are capable.

If you are too ruthless in pruning, you may find your article ends up too short. Lengthening an article needs care or the insertion stands out like a sore thumb. Read your penultimate draft and check what you pruned. Can it be re-inserted without reducing the article's quality? It is often better to re-write a passage rather than to attempt to pad it.

If there appears to be a real problem, go back to your research and see if there is a new aspect which could be inserted with validity.

With experience, the over-shortened piece very rarely occurs, for all writers learn to over-write to allow for pruning.

Reading something repeatedly tends to condition you to the sound of it. You begin to accept it, losing your critical sense. If you have time in hand, put the article away for a few days. Then take it out and read it aloud again. If you still think you can do no better, then the article is finished.

Titles

Sometimes the title of the article comes into my mind during the writing of an article, but often it is left for me to wrestle with at the end. Titles can be a bugbear. I have known some writers who have held back finished work for weeks because they were unable to think of a good title.

What is a good title anyway? Some, of course, are bluntly factual, 'The isle of St Kilda.' Some titles have all the qualities of a good opening paragraph, but in a condensed form. They can be intriguing, controversial, enigmatic, sensational or just plain clever. In other words, they should catch the attention.

If you and your work are unknown to an editor, a feeble title might discourage him from reading on. For this reason alone, it pays to think up the best title you can.

Editors have a nasty habit of dropping your clever title and replacing it with something too awful for words. I can't remember Molly's original title for her 'Fern' article, but anything would have been better than *She*'s own choice – 'Ferny Peculiar!' However, if your market choice likes puns and you can write them – go ahead and give them what they want.

Frankly, I have little talent for titles. I struggle with them until finally I am reduced to offering something very ordinary in the hope that the editor will find something better. 'Root of all evil,' about the mandrake root, was one of my better efforts.

Molly is far better at titles and one I particularly liked was for an article on her efforts as a beginner beekeeper. Headed with a photograph of her in her beekeeper's veil and being crawled over by a mass of bees, her title was 'A novice takes the veil!'

Some of us have that crossword-type mentality which generates good titles, others have not. When you do your market study, don't forget to study the titles as well. Make a note of the really good ones and study the editor's obvious preferences.

Perhaps I have given the impression that writing an article is a very complicated business and this chapter may have put you off a little. Rest assured that most of the steps I have described become almost automatic with experience.

When your article appears in print, read the published form carefully. If it appears to vary obviously from your typescript, study it and learn from it. I am not suggesting that you change your writing style because of the sub-editing of one article, but you can learn a great deal about the likes and dislikes of a particular editor. Check the pattern of the editing, note the details on your records for that magazine. Bear it in mind the next time you write for it and you are a step nearer one editor's idea of perfection.

Chapter Eight

The presentation of the typescript

Whether your article has been written longhand or on the typewriter, it will have to be typed with a conventional layout before being submitted to an editor.

You will find that people like me still talk about 'manuscripts' instead of 'typescripts,' but don't let that fool you. We type our work like anyone else. Old expressions die hard and, for most purposes, the words 'manuscript' and 'typescript' are synonymous.

Typewriters and word-processors
If you have no typewriter, you will have to find someone to type your work for you. This can be fairly expensive, particularly when you may not sell your work eventually. If you really intend to be a writer, then you must have personal access to a typewriter, even if it means buying one.

A growing number of writers use word-processors now. A word-processor is really a computerised electronic typewriter. Don't be put off by the thought of the technology. They are easy to operate.

Prices of word-processors have fallen rapidly in recent times and a model suitable for most purposes can be obtained for well under £500. I have just purchased a new one. It cost less than the model I bought over three years ago, but it is sixteen times more powerful.

I have found that a word-processor considerably increases my output, and its other great virtue is the ease with which work can be revised. It also enables an article to be stored on a small disc, known as a floppy disc, from which it can be extracted, edited and altered to make a new article – all ready for submission to another market with the minimum of work.

For the beginner, I recommend buying a good second-hand typewriter and then moving on to a word-processor when your earnings justify it.

You may not be able to touch-type, but that is not a problem. You could take a touch-typing course. However, one of the fastest typists I ever knew was a novelist with a prodigious output and she only used one finger on each hand. I use two fingers on each hand, with my thumbs for the space-bar. I break no records, but I manage quite well.

If you decide to use a typing agency for your work, do shop around, for their services vary widely in cost and quality. Some agencies offer to correct spelling, grammar and even layout, but I would be wary about them editing your work out of all recognition. Several reasonably priced agencies advertise in the *Contributors' Bulletin* and in *The Author*, the magazine of the Society of Authors.

It is extremely important that your typescript is neat, clean and conventional in presentation. A grubby, dog-eared missive is a clear indication that you are no professional. It also gives the impression that you are careless in your work and that the article has done the rounds of several magazines previously.

Editors have shown me some of the submissions they have had to deal with and, of course, I have seen the work of some of my novice students. Far too many of them are totally unacceptable.

Some writers seem driven to exercise false economies. They use the lightest paper, the oldest ribbons, the narrowest margins and squeeze the last possible word on every page. One dearly loved but eccentric writing friend of ours, not only used one and a half instead of double spacing, but actually cut up his own paper from wallpaper lining. It was only his undoubted writing talent and the demand for his work that enabled him to get away with it.

In the introduction to this book I mentioned my first efforts at writing and my appalling typescripts. I had an old

Royal typewriter. It had one of those black and red ribbons which insisted on typing the characters in black with a neat red top edging. The 'o's and 'e's printed solid blobs because the typeface needed cleaning. The paper I used was so thin that the 'o' often punched a hole right through. I would have typed both sides if the paper hadn't been too thin for me to do so. Nobody told me about the need for double-spacing. I blush at the thought, but I knew no better. I can only wonder at the miracle of those first acceptances. Of one thing I am certain, I could never get away with it today.

Fortunately, it was gently explained to me that, even if my writing skills were modest, I could lift myself above much of the competition by submitting a professional-looking typescript. From then on I vowed that, when my typescripts landed on an editor's desk, they would be indistinguishable from those of a full-time Fleet Street trained professional, in fact they might be even better. I was determined that they would stand out from the competition and demand attention.

The first page of my typescript never had an alteration on it, not even after Tippex, that magical correction fluid, arrived to cover our sins. If I made a mistake on that first page, I re-typed it as many times as necessary to get it perfect. I was less fussy with the subsequent pages, although they were always clean and tidy. I reasoned that if I hadn't managed to grab the editor's attention by the bottom of the first page, then I probably deserved a rejection anyway. If I had hooked him, he would read it, corrections and all.

Of course, the word-processor changed all that and every submission is perfect, unless I actually overlook an error.

For a conventional typescript, you will need white A4 paper, of a weight about 70-80 gsm. Your ribbon must be black and your typeface standard ie, not italic, script or fancy typeface. The fading of a typewriter ribbon sneaks up on you and you often fail to notice it. Keep your eyes open and, the moment it ceases to be dead black, replace it promptly.

The professional layout

Beginners are often advised to leave a wide left-hand margin. Not surprisingly, they ask how wide is wide. Opinions differ and, in any case, it isn't critical. However, if I am giving layout details to beginners, I like to be specific and then let them vary if they wish. So, for my typescript layout I go to the British Standard, using BS5261, Part I, 1975, 'Recommendations for preparation of typescript copy for printing'. This is available from BSI, 2 Park Street, London W1A 2BS. It is the one I use myself and, if you adhere to it, you can't go wrong.

I always use a cover sheet for British markets, but not all writers seem to bother. Type your name and address in the top right-hand corner of the cover sheet. About 120 mm down the page, type the title of your article, centred on the page. Under this type 'by' and under that your name. If you use a pseudonym, put it here, but put your correct name in the top right-hand corner. It is to the latter name that they will make out the cheque.

A little lower on the left, type the approximate number of words. Don't over-estimate. Don't be precise to the last word. For example 950 words is acceptable, but 1,017 is amateurish and should be called 1,000. Below the wordage state the number of photographs or other illustrations which you are enclosing. Under this type the 'rights' you are offering. In Britain, this will usually be 'First British Serial Rights', usually abbreviated to FBSR. The full significance of rights will be dealt with in Chapter 11. The layout of a typical cover-sheet is shown in the diagram.

On the typescript proper the left-hand margin should be 40 mm, the right-hand 25 mm, with 25 mm at the top and bottom also. These margins are essential for editorial alterations and directions to the printer. Double-spacing is used throughout, again to facilitate editing. Only one side of the paper is used.

On the first page of your typescript proper you can, if you wish, repeat your name and address in the top right-hand corner. Personally, I don't bother.

On the first page leave approximately 80 mm from the top

Charles Bloggs,
2, High St.,
Anytown,
Notts.

How to present a typescript

by

Charles Bloggs

2,000 words approx.

FBSR offered.

and type your title again with your name typed underneath, as on the cover sheet. Purists say that you should not type the title in capitals, but this isn't important. One practice which is common with beginners is to underline the title. Underlining is an indication to the printer that something should be set in italics. The editor has to delete all your underlining with a squiggly line. So make it easy for the editor and, in keeping with your desire to appear professional, leave out all underlining throughout the typescript unless it really is your intention that it should be in italics.

Commence your article a double space below your name. Indent three spaces at the beginning of each paragraph. Don't put extra line-spacing between paragraphs. Leave only one space after punctuations, eg commas, stops etc.

At the bottom of each page except the last, type 'mf,' which signifies that 'more follows', indicating to the editor that the page in hand is not the last and there is another somewhere. A typical first page is shown in the diagram.

At the top of page 2 and the subsequent pages, type a key word from the title, eg if the title were 'The life of the frog,' you could type 'frog.' Follow this with the page number in numerals.

On the last page, type the word 'End,' centred under the last line of the typescript. In the bottom right-hand corner of the last page, repeat your name and address.

If you are using a typewriter, keep a carbon copy of the work. Using coloured lightweight bank paper helps to distinguish the copy readily. With a word-processor you will probably keep it on floppy disc, but wise folks also keep a 'hard-copy,' ie a printed copy.

Some writers put a blank sheet of paper after the last sheet of the typescript to protect it. The reasoning is that if the article is rejected, one can retype the cover sheet, replace the backing sheet and the article may be as good as new for sending off elsewhere, thereby saving a re-type.

It is far better to concentrate on making sure it doesn't come back. In any case, if your market research has been sound, your article will have been specifically aimed at one market and there will be few alternatives for which it would be exactly suited.

approx.
80 mms

← 40 mms →   How to present a typescript   ← 25 mms →

by

Charles Bloggs.

Each morning an avalanche of manuscripts descends on the desks of
most editors. Now, editors are human and they don't have time to read
every word they receive. They know the poorly presented manuscript
is the hallmark of inexperience and its contents will probably prove
it. They are aware that the dog-eared offering has almost certainly
been rejected by several editors already, which says little for its
quality. Most important of all, these editors realise that an untidy
manuscript is being submitted by a writer who takes no pride in his
work and hasn't bothered to learn the elements of his craft.

The lesson is a simple one. Learn the basic skills of writing.
Lay out your manuscript in the accepted fashion and make sure it is
clean and not covered in alterations. It is only then that you can
enjoy the confidence of knowing that, when your manuscript lands on
an editor's desk, it will look professional. Most important of all,
it will stand out from most of its competitors and demand attention.

The words 'manuscript' and 'typescript' are synonymous, for all
work must be typed. The ribbon must be black and the typeface
standard. You should use white A4 paper of medium weight, not less
than 70 gms. Lighter paper is a false economy, for it is less
durable and creates a bad impression.

25
mms

mf.

Typescripts which bounce are often returned in a poor state. I often hear complaints of coffee-cup rings and other stains. The best story I heard was from Geoffrey Hemming, the children's writer, who had a typescript returned with a cooked rasher of bacon between the pages – it had obviously fallen out of the editor's bacon sandwich.

I must make it clear that variations on layout are legion and, providing they are not extreme, are accepted by editors fairly happily. Where BS5261 applies, I have quoted it, and where it is inapplicable I have given the details of my own practice. In most respects the layout described for articles also applies to books, for which BS5261 is primarily intended.

Fan-fold paper is commonly used in word-processors, ie paper in one continuous length, with perforations between pages to facilitate separation. It is not British A4, but American A4. This is slightly wider and a little shorter than its British counterpart. I use fan-fold paper exclusively for my typescripts and it appears to be universally acceptable. However, those with typewriters would use British A4.

Some word-processors function on a dot-matrix principle, ie the typed characters are formed by a great number of small dots, which simulates a continuous line in the shape of the required letter. I use a good quality dot-matrix printer and have found this acceptable to all British editors and publishers with whom I had dealings. However, quite a number of American editors state, quite categorically, 'No dot-matrix submissions!' This, I am sure must go back to the days when dot-matrix was poor and the type difficult to read. Modern printers are described as near letter quality and are excellent. However, if you use dot-matrix, such editorial demands can only be ignored at your peril.

Your article is now ready for submission. The typescript, with covering letter and an appropriately stamped, self-addressed envelope should be paper-clipped together, never pinned, stapled or tagged. It is then folded once only and sent off to your chosen market. The details of the covering letter will be dealt with in Chapter 11.

Finally, never sit back and wait for the response. Start work on the next article immediately.

Chapter Nine

Illustrations and their presentation

Illustration research
We have covered market research in some depth, but this
was focused on the text of the article. Now, we must take a
fresh look at the same markets, this time studying the
illustrations.

Although the analysis of illustrations is quite different
from that of the written word, it has the same target of trying
to read the editor's mind and decipher his probable
requirements.

Good illustrations are vital to a magazine's survival. The
eye-catching cover grabs the attention of the bookshop
browser. He thumbs through the pages and sees, not page
after page of boring print, but a balanced collection of
attractive, interesting and intriguing illustrations, interspersed
with text. The layout of a magazine is the product of a
professionally planned balance of photographs, artwork and
text, into which the advertisements are cleverly slotted.

You can safely assume that, unless the piece is very short,
for most magazines your article will require illustrations.
The type of illustrations used will depend on the editor's
judgement, tempered by cost and availability. He may decide
that a photograph would be apt. He might go for one of
those artist's impressions which look almost like photographs
when well done. He might even decide that a cartoon would
best fill the bill.

Picture libraries
Editors have several sources of illustrations open to them.

They may have picture files of their own. For example, some of the country magazines have built up extensive files. Some, indeed, may buy your article but not your pictures, preferring to use their own for economy. Sadly, they are not always better pictures.

Editors also depend heavily on picture libraries and agencies. These have vast collections of first class photographs and other illustrations, but they can be relatively expensive. A brief list of picture libraries can be found in the *Writers' & Artists' Year Book*. The best book on the subject is the *Picture Researcher's Handbook* by Hilary and Mary Evans and Andra Nelki, published by David & Charles.

Cartoons can be commissioned by editors, but their effectiveness depends on the fertility of the cartoonist's imagination and his ability to use the given theme creatively.

Artists' impressions are the work of experts. There may be such talent on the staff of a big magazine, but much of this artwork is done by freelances.

Some magazines have their own photographer. His name may be given with the details of the editorial staff which are usually printed inside the front cover of magazines. More frequently, magazines use freelance photographers who are scattered around the country and on whom they call as needed. In other cases, they may use one or two top-flight photographers who travel the country on a freelance basis.

Recently, a glossy magazine wanted a photograph of me in a specific situation to illustrate one of my articles. I could have agreed to take it myself, but I was very busy and accepted their offer to send a freelance. To my surprise they sent a top man from London, an all-day assignment and a return trip of nearly 300 miles. He told me that the following day he was off on another assignment to Saudi Arabia. The cost to the magazine in his fee and expenses must have far exceeded the amount I had been paid for the article. This indicates the high value that editors often place on illustrations.

Your own photographs
There is, of course, another source of illustrations, namely,

you. If you can supply acceptable illustrations, you will be very popular with most editors. One editor told me, 'When writers send me decent pictures with their articles, they double their chances of acceptance.' Another said, 'Nothing makes me happier than receiving a complete package – words and pictures. Then I don't have to waste time hunting around for illustrations.' Yet another, this time an extreme example, 'I hardly ever accept articles without pictures.' These comments should give the writer a sound incentive to supply his own illustrations, quite apart from the added bonus of being paid twice.

How then should we research the illustrations in magazines? To begin with, look at the proportion of black-and-white to colour. You will find that some magazines can use colour on any page. More cheaply produced magazines confine their colour to a small number of glossy pages, using lower quality paper for pages which carry only black-and-white illustrations and text. In such magazines, your colour illustrations may be squeezed out if there is a demand for remunerative colour advertisements in that issue.

Next, check the relative proportion of photographs, artists' impressions, cartoons and other graphics, eg line drawings, plans, sketches etc.

The function of illustrations

The way illustrations are used is very important. In other words, the function they perform in a specific magazine must be analysed. Look at each illustration and try to identify the reason for its use. Are they eye-catching, even stunning? Are they essential for the proper understanding of the article? For example, in a do-it-yourself article, the construction of a toy might be incomprehensible without several step-by-step photographs or drawings. Ask yourself if illustrations are intriguing or funny, causing the reader to take a second look or give a chuckle. Are they illustrations which, although not essential, nevertheless complement the article and show the reader 'this is what it's like'. Finally, look for those illustrations which I call 'padding pictures' –

those which have no real function other than to break up the monotony of long, dreary-looking expanses of print.

I wrote an article for a medical magazine on 'Alcoholism in industry.' The editor phoned me, 'I need two pictures to break up the text – any pictures!' I scratched my head, but finally came up with two shots of operatives handling machinery in heavy industry. My captions outlined the potential danger of alcoholics in such industrial situations. I blocked out the individuals' faces because I didn't want them to be suspected of being alcoholics. It had the useful double function of implying they were alcoholics. Neither picture was in any way necessary for understanding the article. They were 'padding pictures' and nothing more. Both were accepted and used. Furthermore they are both still on file and have been sold a number of times since.

When studying photographs in magazines, check if the name of the photographer appears. You may find it in very small print under or even up the side of the illustration. Sometimes it will give the name of an agency, such as Popperfoto, BBC Hulton Picture Library, Kobal Collection etc. This gives an insight into the editor's preferred picture sources.

Picture requirements

Whatever the source of the illustrations, editors will have specific requirements. Black-and-white photographs should be on glossy paper, size 10 × 8 inches. They should be sharp with a good range of tones and should be borderless.

The long-established practice of magazines was only to accept colour transparencies and never colour prints for colour illustrations. However, that has been changing. The top quality markets still insist on transparencies, but many down-market magazines using lower quality paper are finding it less expensive to use good colour prints. This also applies to those newspapers which use colour.

Because colour prints restrict the available markets, the astute writer/photographer will normally use transparencies. Before offering colour prints, always check with the editor. Most magazines accept 35 mm transparencies, but a few ask for 6 × 6 cm minimum, particularly for cover shots.

All photographs must carry your name and address and must be captioned. For the black-and-white, the name and address can be lightly written on the back, but there is danger of it coming through on the front. In addition, a great deal of photographic printing is done on resin-coated paper which does not absorb most inks. You can find the ink on the back of one print coming off on the face of another.

I use a rubber-stamp stating 'Copyright' and giving my name and address. It is used with a spirit-based inking pad which is satisfactory with resin-coated paper. An alternative is the popular peel-off label.

Slides should have your name and address written with a fine permanent-ink pen on the plastic slide-mount. If there is insufficient room, put name and phone number only.

Captioning

Captioning is an art in its own right. Newspapers usually want the facts portrayed in the photograph and also the date it was taken. Magazines prefer a caption which encapsulates the facts in a pithy way, which requires skills similar to titling.

Again, study the market and check the editor's preference. There are those pictures that tell their own story and need no caption; indeed, a caption would be gilding the lily and would spoil the effect. Some editors like a few terse words. Others go for the longer caption.

Sometimes a short piece of, say, 100-200 words can be built round a picture – the caption becoming a filler or a short-short. Market research will tell you when editors use this type of piece. Typical of the filler market would be the illustrated letters from readers used by *The Field* and *Country Life*. They are not very well paid, but may be worth making an extra print for, if a picture is being printed for an article elsewhere. However, you should only submit those which you think are sure-fire winners. One or two rejections make the overall remuneration not worth the trouble.

Longer pieces are a far better proposition. For example, I was photographing the Pembrokeshire coast and came across a primitive little harbour. The entrance was narrow and guarded by jagged rocks. Although there was an off-shore wind, the entrance was white with foam and appeared a very dangerous place indeed. The two or three little boats moored there looked most vulnerable. It was overcast and the light poor. Many would have ignored the gloomy scene and carried on.

I took a black-and-white shot from high on the cliffs, showing the harbour, boats and entrance, all in the most dramatic light. With a brief homily on the need for local knowledge before trying to enter such places, I sold it for a satisfying fee to the *Practical Boat Owner*.

There are two commonly used methods for captioning black-and-white prints. In both cases you type your caption on a strip of paper. Some prefer to attach the strip to the back of the print, using a couple of tabs of cellotape. Others attach it with a length of cellotape, again on the back of the print, but hanging down like a flap so that it can be read from the front.

Captioning colour transparencies is more difficult. I attach a tiny circular red peel-off label to each mount I am submitting and number them in sequence. I then type a separate sheet with the numbers against the captions. All my transparencies have a serial number on them in my own code, which identifies them in my filing system and gives the last two figures of the year they were taken. I put this serial number in brackets against the caption, just in case the circular label comes off. The reason I don't use the serial numbers only is that they are often similar and the eye-catching red label with its single number makes it easy for the editor.

Larger transparencies, such as 6×6 cm, are unmounted and should be in separate transparent envelopes with the number on the outside in permanent ink. Also write your name and address on each envelope. Again, the captions are typed on a separate sheet.

Packaging

It is important that illustrations should reach the editor in perfect condition and, hopefully that they should return to you in the same state. Packaging is, therefore, very important. Many writers use the photographic envelopes which have a single sheet of thin cardboard forming the back. I have had too many pictures creased and damaged in these envelopes and consider them unacceptable. I use two pieces of thin corrugated cardboard, cut neatly to size with the corrugations going at right angles to each other, rather like plywood. I hinge them together along one side, using masking tape, place my pictures inside and hold the package closed with a couple of elastic bands. I have printed labels with my name and address and the message, 'Please use packing for return of photographic material'. I stick one of these to the cardboard.

Slides must be handled differently. Never send glass-mounted slides. They get broken and editors hate them. For packing slides, I use plastic wallets with individual pockets for each slide. These are obtainable cheaply from advertisers in the popular photographic press. Again, make sure your name and address are on the outside of the wallet. You can cut down the wallets to smaller sizes if you are only sending a few slides. One sheet of cardboard is sufficient to reinforce the package as the slide mounts provide their own rigidity.

Envelopes should carry a label, 'Photographs, please do not bend.' The SAE accompanying photographs should have the same label and should, of course, have sufficient postage to cover the return. Valuable original slides should always be sent by registered post.

Graphics
Simple graphics in the shape of line drawings are very easy to produce and within the capabilities of the most ham-fisted of us. For example, I have included the plans for making bat-boxes (the roosting boxes for bats) in articles. They consisted of carefully drawn straight-line diagrams. I used dry-transfer lettering, such as Letraset, to name components, give measurements and to do titles.

There are several tools which make such graphics easier and are well worth buying, if you feel that you will have use for them. The best pens are Rotring, which have interchangeable reservoirs for ink and interchangeable nibs of various sizes. The Rotring drawing board and drawing head are excellent tools. They provide a small equivalent of a draftsman's drawing board and protractor. A set of French curves or one of those clever flexible curve-drawing tools are the only extras you need for simple diagrams.

Use Rotring ink on white drawing paper. You may find that the ink will bleed on ordinary typing paper and give lines which are unsharp. Use A4 paper and draw oversize. It will be reduced in the printing process. Remember that lettering and the thickness of the lines will also be reduced, so allow for this or the result could be spidery.

If you make errors, a useful tip is to use one of the better typing correction fluids to alter it. Then get the finished work photocopied by a good quality copying service. The corrections will be invisible.

There is no real substitute for being your own photographer, but if you are not prepared to undertake this, there is an alternative which has worked quite well for a number of writers. Contact your local camera club secretary and ask if there is a keen amateur who would be interested in joining forces with a writer. You do the writing, the photographer provides the pictures. If the article sells, you both get paid. If it is rejected, neither of you get anything. So you both work 'on spec.' The easiest way to arrange payment is to ask the editor to pay for writing and illustrations separately. Some, like *The Lady*, do this automatically, if the photographer puts his name and address on the pictures. This happens on the occasions when I illustrate Molly's articles for this market.

Although you may have no inclination to become a photographer, I advise you to read the next chapter carefully. You may well change your mind and feel encouraged to move in to this complementary field. If you do, there is every possibility that it could herald a new upsurge in your writing career. Keep in mind that, unless your article is very short, it will almost certainly require illustration and if you don't supply the pictures, someone else will.

Chapter Ten

Photography for writers

This chapter is mainly concerned with basic guidelines for those writers with little photographic knowledge. It also includes many tips on illustrating articles which could prove valuable to more experienced photographers.

It bears repeating that if article writers are prepared to become competent photographers, they will not only sell more articles, but will also earn more for each article.

Many novices are put off by the apparent complexity of photography, but the advances in technology are such that it has never been easier to take consistently good photographs. Some modern cameras do nearly all the thinking for you, and as long as you are aware of their limitations, they can be relied upon. Fully automatic systems are quite expensive and you can save a great deal by letting your brain take over some of the camera's functions. Not only is there less to go wrong, but you also learn a lot more about photography.

There is no suggestion that you should try to become a Lichfield or a Bailey. You are not aiming at exhibition pictures. Your need is to become a good plain photographer, able to turn out consistent results which simply portray the facts about which you are writing. Along the way you inevitably become better. You acquire an eye for a good picture. You become more selective. You recognise the effectiveness of a certain viewpoint. You know your ability and appreciate your limitations. You will produce the occasional picture which will give you special satisfaction and raise the editor's eyebrows, but your first aim is to climb above mediocrity and that isn't difficult.

Cameras

I have mentioned both 35 mm cameras and those taking 6 ×
6 cm photographs. The former is the workhorse of the
freelance article writer and the latter, known as a medium
format camera, is heavy and expensive and better left until
you really have some need for it.

The most suitable camera for our purpose is undoubtedly
the SLR (single-lens reflex). It is so-called because there is
no separate viewfinder lens and the photographer actually
sees through the same lens which takes the picture.

The 35 mm SLR is very portable, easy and quick to use. It
can carry 36 exposures without reloading the film. It has
another special advantage, that of having interchangeable
lenses, enabling the photographer to select the optimum
lens for the job in hand.

There are a considerable number of reliable makes with
relatively little to choose between them. I have used Olympus
for many years, having had no less than four, none of which
have given me the slightest trouble, despite suffering some
very rough treatment.

I now carry an Olympus OM2 with black-and-white film,
an Olympus OM2 SP with colour slide film and, if I feel it
necessary, an Olympus OM1 as a back-up, usually carrying a
fast colour slide film for poor light conditions.

If you have more than one SLR, make sure you keep to
the same system so that the lenses are interchangeable. This
means you don't need to buy a new camera, merely a
camera body with no lens.

I find I need a medium-format camera for some specialist
jobs. For many years I used a Rolleiflex which I bought for
£60 second-hand. I still have it: it takes beautiful pictures
and is totally reliable. Unfortunately, it doesn't have
interchangeable lenses.

My present medium-format camera is a Hasselblad – a
top quality professional model. It is not the camera to buy
unless you are absolutely certain that photo-journalism is
your game and that such a camera will pay its way. It is not
only expensive, but also very heavy and I don't like using it
unless I can get near my subject by car.

When you buy a new camera, try to find a dealer who is

actually a photographer, not one where the shop assistant also sells videos, cassette recorders and pop records. A true photographic dealer will be helpful, particularly if you run into snags.

Camera clubs

A very good idea for the beginner is to join a local camera club. The details are usually obtainable from the local library. Some camera club members are fanatical about changing their cameras as soon as a new model comes out. This means that it is often possible to pick up a good superceded model in the club for little more than the dealer's trade-in price.

In a camera club you will find guidance and criticism freely given, which can be difficult to obtain elsewhere. Learn as much as you can, but try not to be diverted away from your real purpose and into the realms of artistry.

A book of this nature can do little more than give broad guidance on photography and suggest ways in which the camera can best be used for illustrating articles.

The first step must be to read and understand fully the instruction manual supplied with your camera. If there are points you can't grasp, ask someone – the dealer who sold you the camera, for example.

Learn to hold the camera properly, both for horizontal and vertical shots. Practise squeezing the shutter release rather than jerking it. Make sure you can change shutter speeds and lens apertures with confidence. It is all clearly explained in your manual. Some of these operations may be automatic or semi-automatic, depending on your camera model.

Beginners' faults

Beginners often suffer from faults which are easily remedied. Camera shake is very common. It can be due to incorrect holding, jerking the shutter or using a shutter speed which is too slow. Standing too far away from the subject is another weakness. If, for example, your article is about a country craft, by all means take photographs of the workshop and the craftsman. However, the critical picture, and probably the most saleable, would be a close-up of the craftsman's hands performing the actual task which is the subject of your article. So, when appropriate, get in close and fill your viewfinder with the real subject, not its surroundings.

It is all too easy to be so intent on the subject that the background is ignored. A cluttered background can ruin a picture. You can avoid this in a number of ways. Ensure the subject is against an undistracting background, either by careful posing or by adopting a suitable viewpoint. For example, by simply dropping on one knee the photographer can often outline his subject against the sky. Another frequently used technique is to throw the background out of focus and reduce it to an indistinct blur, by opening the aperture of your lens. However, this also introduces more light to the film and must be compensated by using a faster shutter speed. Again, you will find this technique explained in your manual.

Never rush to buy extra lenses and other equipment until you have found yourself hampered by their absence on several occasions. Most photographers, including me, have expensive lenses which they never use. I suggest that the first extra lens you buy should be a wide-angle lens, probably one of 28 mm. This gives you a wider angle of view, but the subject appears smaller than with your standard lens. It is valuable for use in confined spaces, for example. You will find longer lenses less useful unless you are specialising in wildlife, sport or some similar field. I find a 75-150 mm zoom lens very useful. As its name implies, it is variable between 75 and 150 mm and a good one loses little in quality for having this flexibility. Set at about 110 mm it makes an ideal portrait lens, comfortable for both user and subject and reducing close-up distortion. It is a good lens for the portraits associated with interviewing.

I advise against buying wide angle zoom lenses. They are expensive, quality varies and your need for variability in this range will probably be limited. It is better to stay with a 28 mm prime lens.

For restricted light you will find a flash-gun useful and this will probably be one of your earlier purchases. Buy one that is fairly powerful without being too heavy. Practise using it off the camera. That means operating the camera with one hand, holding the flash-gun high and out to one side with the other. This is easier than it sounds and avoids that frontal lighting which produces such flat uninteresting pictures.

A tripod is a very useful tool, but it is heavy and conspicuous. One thing is sure, you can't sneak around with a tripod taking candid shots. However, its rock-like steadiness improves the work of many photographers beyond recognition, especially if they have shaky hands.

Black-and-white

There is a much bigger market for black-and-white pictures than colour, although the imbalance is slowly decreasing. You will be wise to concentrate on black-and-white for, not only does it suit more markets, it is much cheaper to work with.

For black-and-white, I almost invariably use Ilford FP4 film. This is a medium speed film and is considered too slow for general use by press photographers, but it suits me admirably. It is acknowledged as the best medium-speed film on the market. If light is poor and flash unsuitable, I use Ilford HP5 – a faster film.

Errors in exposure in black-and-white photography can usually be compensated for in the darkroom enlarging process, unless the photo is too far out.

Processing

It is a great advantage if you can develop your own black-and-white film. This is a simple process and doesn't even require a darkroom. With a plastic developing tank, a lightproof changing bag, a thermometer, a few cheap chemicals and access to a sink, you can easily do this. The total cost of such equipment would be about £10 and would pay for itself handsomely. Personal instruction is best, but not essential. Again, your camera club would teach you in a few minutes.

Enlarging requires more equipment and more space with total darkness facilities. It is better deferred until you are sure you want to invest in it. Many camera clubs have darkrooms with enlargers and members only have to pay for the materials they use.

Failing this, a processing service will have to be used.

If you are unable or unwilling to develop your own, there are developing and enlarging services for black-and-white photographs advertised in the back pages of the popular photographic press, of which *Amateur Photographer* is the leader.

Apart from the cheapness, a strong reason for developing your own black-and-white is the convenience of doing so. If you send off a film to be developed, you don't want 10 × 8 enlargements of the 20 or 36 negatives, for that would be prohibitively expensive. The alternative is to wait until the negatives are returned, then select those you want enlarged and send the negatives back again. This takes time and postage. If you develop your own film you can make your choice on the spot and then send off only the preferred negatives for enlargements.

Colour
Inevitably you will eventually move on to colour for some of your work. Colour photography is more critical and unforgiving of even small errors. The same rules of sharpness and composition apply, but there is little margin for error in exposure. Editors demand what is called full colour saturation, which means strong colours with no hint of over exposure. If uncertain about an important shot, you can hedge your bets by what is known as 'bracketing.' This means you take your shot at what you believe to be the optimum exposure. Then take at least two more shots, one with a half or whole stop more exposure and another with a half or whole stop less. One of them should turn out to be spot on.

Few article writers develop their own colour film. I don't. I use Kodachrome 64 for most purposes, with Kodachrome 25 for fine work. Both of these films are processed by Kodak and the cost of processing is included in the purchase price.

In the medium format, 120 size film is used and this is not available in Kodachrome, although its coming is often rumoured. I use Ektachrome and this is not process-paid and must be sent to a laboratory for processing.

When you start out in the field, think back to your illustration market study. What did the photographs in the magazine look like? Think of how the subject filled the picture – the viewpoint – the background. What did the photographer appear to be aiming at? Why did it appeal to the editor? Keep these points in your mind's eye as you compose your pictures.

Look for interesting viewpoints, but remember that your subject comes first. You aren't looking for breathtaking results, but a picture to tell your story. For example, the licensee of a local off-licence was fed up with a window full of posters giving special offers. It was a sunny window and so he bought some tomato plants and put them in the window. By skill and good fortune they grew superbly. People started coming in to ask for growing advice. His sales boomed. I took a photograph, wrote up a piece and sold it to *Off-licence News*. The editor wasn't interested in an artistic photograph with delightful cloud effects. He wanted a full-frontal picture of the shop, showing the name and the tomatoes. That is exactly what he got. So be careful – in many cases your prime purpose is to show the facts, not your artistic talent, but if the two can be combined, so much the better.

When you are photographing to illustrate an article, don't stick to the obvious viewpoint, vary it a little and shoot more film than you think you will need. This not only gives you a better selection, but also enables you to offer exclusive shots with re-writes of the article to other magazines.

An example of this was when I was asked to cover a devastating breach of a canal bank. I photographed the resulting crater from both sides to give entirely different viewpoints for two magazines, but I wanted to write it up for a third market also. To get another shot I went a mile or so up the canal to the point where navigation had been stopped. I took a shot looking through a very photogenic bridge, including the notice saying 'No navigation beyond this point' and the sweep of a lovely canal reach stretching into the distance. The caption stressed that the most tantalising aspect of the canal was inaccessible, due to the breach. All three sold, complete with pictures.

A point about technique here. In order to get the foreground, the notice, and the distant background all in focus, I had to shut down my lens to a very small aperture. This effectively increased my depth of field, bringing it all into focus. It also greatly reduced the amount of light reaching the film. To compensate, I had to use a much slower shutter speed. The slow shutter speed meant that it would be difficult to hold the camera and avoid shake, so I used a tripod. This is an obvious technique to most photographers, but I mention it to show beginners that photography is often a matter of achieving a compromise between a number of variable factors.

On the subject of taking extra shots, it is worth mentioning that editors don't always know what they want. For example, I was asked by an editor to get a colour photograph of a personality, and, among other requirements, to make sure that some local spectacular scenery was seen in the background. The requirements were too tight to be practical, but he wanted them so I did as he asked. I then took a couple of shots as I thought it should be done and sent those to the editor as well. He used my choice – very wisely I thought. So never be afraid of shooting a couple of extra off-beat shots, you might come up with a winner.

'Mug shots'

Editors will sometimes ask for a photograph of yourself – what the Americans call 'mug shots.' Trade and professional magazines particularly like them.

You can take these shots yourself, using the timer on your camera or you can get someone else to press the release. It is wise to have a few of these pictures taken of you in various situations and wearing different clothes. Obviously, a shot of you in formal attire behind a desk is inappropriate for an article on 'How to build a dry-stone wall' and a shot in a bikini just wouldn't do for 'How to re-negotiate your mortgage.'

The saying that we measure our freedom by those things we can do without applies very aptly to photography. Too often we weigh ourselves down with cameras, lenses, flashguns and tripods, most of which we are unlikely to use, until we can hardly move. I am as guilty as anyone. My Hasselblad outfit with tripod weighs a crippling 12 kilos. As I very rarely take it without also taking my 35 mm cameras as well, it begins to overflow on to Molly's patient shoulders. If I am on my own, I have to start some ruthless load-shedding before I can consider myself mobile at all.

So bear in mind that equipment must be carried and that weight can be a vital factor. This is particularly important for travel photographers.

When you go on a photographic sortie, always take spare camera batteries, flashgun batteries and plenty of film. Unless I am going on a trip where I expect to use a lot of film, I prefer the 20 exposure cassettes (recently changed to 24 exposures) in Kodachrome, rather than the 36 exposure. I hate having to waste a lot of film in order to get a few shots processed.

In black-and-white I buy my film in bulk, 30 metres at a time, and fill my own cassettes with whatever length I require.

Finally, if you are a photographer, re-read the preceding tips and be determined to slant your work to the special needs of the article market. If you are a beginner I repeat yet again, think very seriously about taking up photography, for it can open an entirely new world for you in the field of article-writing.

Chapter Eleven

Selling your work

Many writers are so occupied with the practice of writing that they pay little attention to the selling of their work. That can be a serious and expensive mistake.

If you write solely for pleasure, then you can skip this chapter, but I still advise you to read it. It could make you change your mind. For those who are serious about their work and expect to be paid for it, this chapter is essential reading.

I know writers who feel so vulnerable at the thought of handing over their brainchild to a merciless editor, that they can hardly bear to do so.

I once listened to the members of a Writer's Circle reading their work for constructive criticism. Some efforts were poor, the majority were mediocre, but a few were good. Of these, one was outstanding. Here, I thought, is real talent. I went up to the writer afterwards and asked if the piece had been published. She told me that she had no idea where to send it. I gave her a magazine and an editor's name who, I believed, would snap it up.

About a year later I bumped into her. 'Did he buy your piece?' I asked.

She blushed, 'I haven't got round to sending it yet.'

Obviously, you must get your work into an editor's hands before he can think of buying it. You must get it into the right hands, often at the right time and you must have a sales strategy which gives you the maximum chance of a sale at the best fee you can achieve.

I enjoy writing, but I set a value on it – the value of both my skill and time. Many beginners are so anxious to see themselves in print that they are prepared to accept little or nothing for the privilege. This is fair enough during your apprenticeship; unfortunately a small number of editors trade on it.

I remember tutoring a writing course, not many years ago. I was looking around for markets for the students' class work, much of which was saleable. I phoned the local county magazine, explaining my interest and asking their rates.

'We pay £1.05p per thousand words.'

'Not to my students!' I replied.

'Most people are only too glad to have their work published,' was the cold response.

It is a sad fact that there will always be people who will write for virtually nothing or even pay to get published. The important point is that you must not be one of them. If you are taking the trouble to try to write professionally, then you must sell professionally.

You may have a high opinion of your work. Your family and friends may praise it to the skies, but you will never know its true quality until the day when someone is prepared to dig into their pockets, and dig deeply, to pay for it.

Query letters

How should you go about selling your work? You will have done your careful market research and discovered the best magazine for your purpose, one with at least reasonable rates. We must presume, of course, that you have something worth selling. You now write a carefully worded query letter to the editor.

There are people who will tell you that query letters are a waste of time and postage. Don't believe it. They are wrong. For article-writers, query letters are great savers of time and money and are the best route to acceptance.

Query letters should be brief and to the point. They should be addressed to the editor or, in the case of larger editorial departments, to the features editor.

Never address the editor as 'Dear Sir,' 'Dear Madam,' 'Dear Sir/Madam' or even 'Dear Editor.' It is amateurish and clearly shows that you haven't bothered to read a recent issue of the magazine or even to glance at it in a bookshop. If you have done your market research, you know the editor's name.

One editor actually stated that nothing irritated him more than receiving letters addressed to his predecessor. Petty perhaps, but can you afford to ignore such things?

The correct form of address is 'Dear Mr . . .' or 'Dear Ms . . . .' Magazines never indicate the marital status of their female staff, so unless you happen to know, from correspondence, that 'Miss' or 'Mrs' is preferred, 'Ms' is the title to use.

Whilst verifying the current editor's name in the bookshop, also check that the address is the same as on your own files. They do change.

I live in the country and a long way from a large bookshop. If I am writing for a magazine after a lapse of time, I phone the magazine and check with the operator on the switchboard. 'Is Mr . . . still the editor of *Tiddley-winks Weekly*, please?' I also ask if the address has changed. The call is brief, costs only a few pence and ensures that I am right up to date.

Address the editor by name. Ask bluntly if he would be interested in an article on . . . Briefly state any reasons why he should be interested, eg an unusual aspect, topicality, an association with a big name – anything which may hook his attention – but keep it brief. Add, also briefly, any way in which you are qualified to write the article, if indeed you are so qualified. State any illustrations which you could supply. Ask how many words he would like to see, if interested. Enclose a stamped, addressed envelope.

Query letters to foreign markets require International Reply Coupons (IRCs), obtainable from your local Post Office. Details of IRC's are given in Chapter 4 on Market Research.

Our main overseas market is America. We find American editors are, generally speaking, tougher than their UK counterparts. One aspect which we find particularly irritating is, if American editors are disinterested in your query, they often fail to reply, despite the IRC's – a practice fairly rare in UK editors, but by no means unknown.

One word of warning – never make a firm offer of something which you may not be able to deliver. You can, of course, qualify an offer by saying, for example, 'I hope to arrange to camp on Rockall for a week. Would an article on my experiences interest you?' Clearly, such a trip could fall through for a variety of reasons.

There are a few articles for which query letters are often inappropriate. Humour is one of them. Unless the editor knows you and your work, it will be impossible for him to assess the value of a humorous article without seeing it. Another case would be the subject which is difficult to describe without a letter nearly as long as the article itself. Query letters are hardly worthwhile for short-shorts, but the truly professional article-writer rarely bothers with this field of writing anyway.

We rarely write an article without a query letter or, in the case of a regular market, a phone-call. Believe me, the policy pays off handsomely.

To summarise the benefits of query letters:
1. They save time and money in writing for a market which:
    (a) Has just published such an article.
    (b) Has a similar article in the pipe-line.
    (c) Finds the proposed length quite unsuitable.
    (d) Is not interested in the subject.
2. Query letters discover editors' up to date length requirements.
3. Query letters can stimulate editorial interest. Declared interest is nearly as valuable as a commission.

If the editor replies declining the suggestion, you find another market and repeat your query.

If the editor expresses interest, note the number of words he suggests and any other points he may make. Now write the article promptly to the required length.

When the article is submitted, enclose a brief covering letter, thanking him for his letter, quoting its date and any reference. Make the point that he asked to see your article.

It is important to get the article off as quickly as possible. He might just remember your query, but he will be unimpressed if you refer to his letter of three months earlier. Also, someone could have pipped you to the post.

Sometimes editors will ask you to change part of your article, to alter the slant perhaps. Do this immediately and return it, thanking him for his valuable suggestion and acknowledge the improvement, even if you do so with your tongue in your cheek. He can hardly turn the altered work down, after all he will feel he half wrote it himself.

Holding on to markets

When you have a piece accepted by an editor, hang on to him, but don't swamp him. Follow your success up with another query letter, not forgetting to refer to your acceptance so that he remembers who you are. I say something like, 'Glad you liked the piece on . . .' or 'I enjoyed your presentation of my piece on . . . in August's issue,' or 'Thank you for your cheque for my last article.' This establishes your credentials. He accepted your work once, which means that you can write to his satisfaction. He will at least read your query carefully.

Editors frequently move. When editors change, contact the new one with a query, making sure you refer to your past acceptances. Ring up the magazine's switchboard and ask the operator where the previous editor has gone. The chances are that he has moved to another magazine, possibly an up-market one which might pay you even better. Write him a query letter and thank him for his past co-operation, wish him luck in the new job and express the hope that you can still write for him. With a little good fortune, your single market has become two.

Multiple submissions

Research is time-consuming. It is vital that you use your research material as economically as possible. I have even heard of an article-writer who had no interest in a subject unless he could see the possibility of at least twenty sales from it. That requires a lot of know-how, but half-a-dozen should be a fairly easy target at which to aim.

How do you handle multiple submissions without treading on editorial toes and getting into people's black books? Firstly, I am not talking about multiple submissions of the same article. They are the same subject, probably using some common material, plus some that is new. They will probably have a different slant and they will almost certainly be sold to non-rival publications or, at least, sold some months apart.

Take the article on Geoffrey Ball, the pilot turned charcoal-burner. His story could have been keyed to his RAF exploits, his farming or his civil aviation, all of which would have culminated in his charcoal-burning. Changing slants and changing emphasis alters the article.

In fact, his story was sold to a number of general interest magazines in various forms. In addition, *Choice* with their series on starting second careers later in life, was an obvious outlet. They took an article stressing this aspect. Charcoal is a form of solid fuel, so the trade magazine, *Solid Fuel*, bought an article on the charcoal-burning aspect. As Geoffrey used forestry trimmings in his kilns, it was easy to sell an article to *Forestry and British Timber*.

One of Molly's specialities is the coffee-houses of old Georgian and Queen Anne London. She has sold articles on them to a great number of general interest magazines. Her trade and house magazine sales include the glossy magazines of hotel chains, the prestigious world-wide coffee trade magazine *Coffee International* and, because London coffee houses were the forerunners of our postal services, she sold a piece to the *Post Office Courier*.

We both write on bats. Apart from the general interest and nature magazines, we have written for the most unlikely outlets. I have already described how I linked bats with caravans. The magazine *Exchange Contracts*, which is a free handout in solicitors' offices to those contemplating house purchase, took an article. It was based on advice to those who buy a new house and find they have bats.

Many species of bats live in trees and so *Forestry & British Timber* bought an article. *Farmers Weekly* not only took an article, but invited me to brief their editor on bats for a TV programme.

Well-captioned bat pictures have sold to numerous magazines and books, including unexpected outlets like *Junior Education* and *The Master Builder*.

These examples should be sufficient to show you that a great deal of mileage can be obtained from sound research, constantly updated. Once you have written several articles on a subject, you will probably find that you can write them off the top of your head with very little reference. This is a great time-saver and therefore a money spinner. It should be evident that it makes sound writing sense to look out for those subjects which have this multiple sales potential.

Commissions

Until you become well known to an editor, you are unlikely to be offered commissions. However, it does happen and I have been given commissions for markets for which I have never previously written, but I have always made my past track-record clear.

Sometimes you may get an idea for a series of articles on related themes. If so, explain your idea briefly when you send the query letter. Offer to include a list of proposed titles when you send the first article. If the editor likes the idea and the first article, he may commission the rest.

If you are commissioned and your commissioned work doesn't satisfy the editor he will reject it, although he might ask for a re-write. In the case of rejection, he may offer you a 'kill' fee. This is a percentage of what you would have received had the article been accepted. The proportion varies from magazine to magazine and, indeed, some pay no kill fees.

If no kill fee is offered, then you should ask for it. Write to the editor, saying that you are sorry he is unable to accept the article, but would he kindly pay you his usual kill fee. Bear in mind that the rejection may not have been because the article was sub-standard, but there may have been a change in policy or a cut-back. Of course, he may ignore your request. However, for most writers the rejection of a commission is an extreme rarity.

Expenses
Sometimes you can get expenses out of an editor for a commissioned article; much depends on your standing with him. Travelling and subsistence are reasonable expenses, but not all magazines will pay them, even on commissioned work. Other expenses are a matter for prior negotiation with the editor. For example, I suggested to a caravanning magazine that they should pay my expenses to attend a caravanning course as a 'guinea-pig'. They agreed and commissioned the article. I attended the weekend course, obtained plenty of material and took sufficient photographs. The article was accepted and duly paid for. I then re-wrote the article for *Choice*, making the point that many people start caravanning on retirement. How do they begin? Are courses on caravanning worthwhile? The Caravan Club saw the article in *Choice*, liked it and bought the Second British Serial Rights without my having to write another word. The pictures which had illustrated the articles have sold a number of times elsewhere. All in all, not a bad outcome for an enjoyable and instructive weekend, with all expenses paid. However, with such commissions always clear with the editor in advance that the copyright of the photographs remains yours.

Sometimes, commissions go wrong. I had commissions to write a number of articles on specific scenes in the Highlands for an American magazine. Unless it is a brief trip, I use the caravan as a base. From the outset, the weather was appalling. It varied between mist, rain and howling gales and finally I had to give in and return. We had been washed out and battered by storms, with only one short blink of sunshine the whole time. As my market insisted on colour photographs in bright weather, I was almost empty-handed.

I explained the problem to the editor who was understanding. However, I had driven over 1,600 miles and had quite an outlay invested in the trip. I recouped some of this by drawing on my experiences in remote hilly places in really bad weather. My articles on 'Handling caravans in high winds' and 'Handling caravans on hills' sold to two different magazines.

I had one excellent colour shot which was used by a magazine, blown up to cover two whole pages. My stormy black-and-white pictures are on file for future use. In this way I was able to make capital from what some would have accepted as a total loss. It proves that it is important to keep your eyes open and, if possible, to have contingency plans in case things don't go the way you anticipate.

Contact with editors

A few editors welcome phone calls, but most of them find them an irritation. Only phone if you have something requiring an urgent decision – a scoop or something topical. Scoops come rarely, but remember that, if you have something really good, you can ring a national newspaper with a reverse charge call and ask for the news-desk. If they want it, they will pay for it. Have it ready to dictate and don't forget to give your name and address.

Magazines work so far ahead that pieces of immediate topicality are of no interest to them.

If you have been writing for an editor for some time, it is worth asking for a higher rate. At the worst, the editor can only refuse. One editor told me, quite frankly, 'I have two main rates, the top one for professionals and the lower one for the part-timer.' From then on I got the top rate – another good reason for acting professionally in approach and presentation.

One national magazine quoted me firm fees for its various requirements. Imagine my shock when I found that one of my students had been paid a fee far in excess of mine, and that for only preparing a factual draft. He was, it is true, an expert in his field and his information was vital to the credibility of the article. If you are fortunate enough to be an expert, make sure the editor knows it.

A word of caution. Don't be too free in telling people the fees you are paid. The quality of your work may merit you a higher rate because it needs little sub-editing. Tell that to another writer and he may be complaining to the editor to your disadvantage. That is why you will find that I have quoted no specific fees for publications in this book. In any case, such figures would be out of date before publication.

As you build a good relationship with an editor, you may feel like calling to see him. This can be quite useful, but never go without an appointment. If he sounds less than enthusiastic, drop the idea.

When you call, make sure you have something to offer. Never go expecting a chat. I once had appointments to see the editors of two London national magazines in the same morning. I called on each and made my sales pitch. I knew exactly what I proposed to offer each one. One gave me coffee, the other was too busy even to offer, but I came away with three commissions from each. If you call, say your piece and leave. Never overstay your welcome.

Agents

Beginners often ask if they should use an agent. The answer is that the problem doesn't really arise. Few, if any agents will handle articles, unless you are on their books for your full-length works. I have used agents for foreign sales with mixed results. If you make a real success of your article-writing and want to sell worldwide, then I suggest that syndication might be worth considering. They will market your work worldwide and charge a commission. The addresses of a number of syndication agencies are given in the *Writers' & Artists' Yearbook*.

Sharp practices

A chapter on selling is probably the appropriate place to mention the problems of non-payment, sharp practices and general chicanery, in which the writing world differs little from any other.

In a delightful lecture at the Writers' Summer School on 'The conflict and challenge of a writer's priorities,' William Horwood advised us never to treat our publisher like a friend, a parent or a grandfather. 'For,' he said, 'he is a crook, a very clever crook.' It was said with the tongue in the cheek, but I am sure he would have included editors as well.

I have had a director of a major publishing house leave the company taking my book material with him. It was years before I was able to recover it and I know I probably lost a great deal of money over it.

One editor owed me a considerable sum in expenses. It took pressure via the Society of Authors finally to recover it some two years later. The same editor offered me £100 over the phone for a short piece and then sent me a cheque for £60. His excuse was that he had forgotten how much he had offered me on the phone.

One magazine published an illustrated article of mine. About a year later I discovered one of my illustrations used again, this time gracing someone else's article. My letter to the editor brought a cheque and a note saying, 'Thank you for reminding me.'

Geoffrey Hemming, whose talented 'How to make your own toys' articles for children have been published world-wide, told me that his work is often stolen. Whilst holidaying up north, he glanced at a local newspaper and found one of his articles, blatantly including his own meticulously drawn illustrations. He wrote an irate letter to the editor and, by return received a cheque, but no word of explanation or apology.

Clearly, such editors recognise the odds are in their favour and, if they only get caught out once in every ten occasions, they are slashing the fees they have to pay by 90%. Some call it piracy, but just plain stealing is good enough.

A few magazines pay on acceptance, but most pay on publication. You can wait months and even years for your money. It is an accepted practice but a strange one. One could buy no other commodity and offer to pay for it only when you decide actually to use it.

Before you begin to think that editors are all criminals, I must reassure you. The majority of them are decent hard-working folk who are just doing their job. Very few of them will steal your ideas, pirate your work, hang on to your fees or filch your photographs. They are, however, in business to

95

get results. Even if you are on Christian name terms with them, don't expect them to buy your work for 'auld lang syne.' They will buy your articles because they meet their current requirements and for no other reason. Remember, editors survive in their jobs by the sales of their publications. It is the quality of your work, and writing like it, which ultimately controls circulation figures. Editors are not philanthropists, nor can you expect them to be.

Earlier I mentioned that I have had only two rejections in recent years. The first was for an American magazine and, although no explanation was offered in their letter, I have a feeling I was trying to ape the American style too closely. In other words, I was writing out of character.

In the second case it was entirely my own fault. I had sent a query letter and received a go-ahead, with the editor agreeing to wait until my book on the same subject was published. This would give the book valuable publicity.

When the book was launched, I found myself very heavily committed to promotion appearances and I was run off my feet. The article was written in desperate haste and I broke one of my cardinal rules. 'If the article doesn't satisfy you, don't send it.' It didn't satisfy me, but I sent it.

I fully deserved to have it back from an editor who knew my work and had expected something better. His cold note said, 'Your article is informative, but little more.' I had marshalled my facts and written my article, but it had no life in it. I had let down both the editor and myself and he could no longer take the quality of my work for granted.

The magazine was an upmarket one for which I had written with no problems in the past. It will take some time for me to restore that editor's confidence in me. Yet this salutary lesson did me good. It brought me up with a jolt and made me vow never to fall into the same trap again. You will be well advised to learn from it also.

Rights

The expression 'rights' has been mentioned several times. This refers to the right to use your work which you are offering a publication, probably with certain limitations.

The one most commonly used in UK is 'First British Serial Rights' (FBSR). This means that the magazine is being offered the right to publish this piece once and for the first time in Britain. The word 'serial' does not mean that it will appear in serial form, but that the magazine is published on a periodic basis.

Second British Serial Rights can be sold and even Third and subsequent rights also. In practice, this rarely happens, for shrewd writers merely re-write the first article to change it materially and then sell the First Rights again. There are good reasons for this. For one thing, subsequent rights bring in a lower fee and also they are less attractive to editors. They can also cause complications and embarrassments. For example, you may sell the first rights to a magazine which holds on to the article. Then you sell the second rights to a magazine which publishes promptly. The second magazine has in effect obtained the first rights and the first magazine has been left with the second. The answer is that, on the rare occasions when you are asked for the second serial rights, first make sure that the magazine which has bought the first rights in the article has actually published it.

If you sell the First British Serial Rights, you are perfectly free to sell foreign rights, eg First North American Serial Rights (the rates, incidentally, are usually better.)

Some editors are notorious for ignoring the rights you offer and trying to force a deal for all rights. Some even pay you by cheque, requiring your endorsement on the back agreeing to give them all rights. This is a try-on. You have made your offer, so stick to it. Send the cheque back and ask for it to be altered in keeping with the rights you offered.

Books from articles
Articles can be excellent stepping-stones to non-fiction books on the same subject. You will have done much of the research already. Even more important, you will have something to show the publisher to prove that, not only do you know your subject, but you can actually write.

I have had two book contracts based solely on my articles.

This proved so easy that I am now using this as a sales strategy for future books.

For full details on writing and selling non-fiction books, together with their development from articles, see my companion book, *The Way to Write Non-fiction*, in the same series.

'Freebies'

I am often asked about the fringe benefits which come the way of writers – what the Americans call 'freebies.' The answer is that they don't come very often, particularly to beginners. I have never been offered the luxury cruise of which some writers boast. I have had press lunches, some excellent and some indifferent. I have had products to test and to keep. I have even had a free full medical overhaul with all the latest electronic gadgetry. I have also enjoyed an hour's float in silence and total darkness in a sealed bath of concentrated Epsom salts, but that is another story.

Get known. Use publicity. Sell yourself. It brings work as well as freebies. I have had five TV appearances and six radio broadcasts in the last six months. I have more to come, including a TV documentary. Not everyone enjoys the undoubted pressure of this type of work, but it does pay off and you meet some interesting people.

Finally, be professional in your work and your sales. You will find it will bring you benefits in both status and income.

98

Chapter Twelve

Specialised writing

Being a specialist

I have already outlined some of the advantages of writing on those subjects in which you have some expertise. So many beginners bow to the advice of 'write what you know about,' that it is important to look at the snags as well.

Having all your eggs in one basket can obviously be risky. I specialise in several fields and most of these have gone through cycles of decline from time to time.

One of my specialist subjects is bats. Until recently, few people knew anything about them apart from their horror-film image. Certainly, very little was written about them. I had the field almost to myself. Then the Wildlife & Countryside Act, 1981, made the bat the most protected animal in Britain. This was followed by 1986 being designated National Bat Year. The spotlight became sharply focused on bats. Bat Groups were formed nationwide and, suddenly, everyone was writing about bats. My near monopoly vanished.

I write for a wide range of medical magazines. The income of such magazines was mainly derived from the advertising of the giant drug companies and the rates paid to writers were good. Government legislation was introduced to control drug company advertising. Magazines were cut-back severely and some even disappeared altogether.

One medical magazine had been buying every single thing I offered them and, when it folded, its loss was a blow. So, another specialisation of mine had been drastically reduced.

These are two examples of the way markets can vanish and they highlight the dangers of being too narrow in your specialisation. By all means begin by writing what you know about. Continue specialising in this subject if it is profitable, but also play the field and, if possible, try to find several special subjects to develop.

Humour

There are quite a number of special writing fields for which some people find they have a talent. Humour is one of these. If you can write humorous articles which tickle an editor or two, you are very fortunate. It is a rare writing quality and one which is much sought after by a surprisingly wide range of magazines. It's also a very subjective thing – what will please one editor will leave another cold. The verbal funnyman is rarely able to express himself on paper, so because you can crack a good joke don't expect instant success as a humorous writer.

Although I sometimes introduce humour into an article, I have never even tried to write a full-length humorous article. They are just not my field.

Writing for children

Children's articles is another special field. Some writers find it so rewarding in every respect, that they write nothing else. The market is wide. Apart from the children's comics and magazines, a great number of newspapers and adult magazines carry children's pages. These sometimes have regular columns for children, which are not out of reach of the freelance.

There is quite an opening for informative articles for children on history, science, natural history and general knowledge, with a growing demand for articles on life-skills.

In this market, the age group, style and presentation vary so widely that it is very important to study all the children's material you can.

A common mistake of aspiring writers for children is to write down to them. It is essential still to have some of the child in you and to at least make an effort to see your writing as if through the eyes of a child.

A visit to the library and a chat with the librarian about the most popular children's books can pay off. It will give you an idea of the subjects which children are finding currently appealing.

Although it deals primarily with fiction, *The Way To Write For Children* by Joan Aiken (Elm Tree Books) gives a valuable insight into this field for those who are interested.

There are some new and growing fields which have an insatiable demand for material. These include the pop scene and computers. If you have special knowledge in these subjects they could pay off extremely well.

Radio

Radio offers a number of slots for the article-writer, but it needs special study, a lot of radio listening and a knowledge of the BBC's specific requirements. The BBC book, *Writing for the BBC*, is the best source of information. It is described as a guide for professional and part-time writers on possible markets for their work within the BBC.

Travel writing

When I am speaking about specialisation, the subject which is raised more often than any other is travel writing. It sometimes appears that half the novice writers I meet aspire to become travel writers and the other half want to write Mills & Boon romances. For this reason, travel writing is worth a special mention, even if only to sound a note of caution.

Travel writing covers a very wide field. It ranges from the occasional piece generated by the annual holiday to the tough and demanding world of the professional travel writer. The latter can make a very good living, but usually earns every penny of it.

Firstly, to be a travel writer and not also be a photographer is an almost impossible role. Every travel writer I know is at least competent with a camera and some of them are first-class photographers.

The market for travel articles is vast, including all the

101

general and women's magazines. There is a growing number of magazines which deal with holidays per se, plus such specialised forms of holidays as time-sharing. In considering the markets you must remember camping, caravanning, motoring, sailing, walking, back-packing and the host of other magazines which, in some form or other, deal with getting around to new places.

You may write on travel, but that doesn't make you a full-blown travel writer. Real travel writing is a hard nut to crack on a full-time basis and you have to be good. Travel writers are usually a dedicated, hard-working bunch, spending weeks of the year cooped up in planes, airport lounges and hotel bedrooms. It is not the glamorous occupation that many think and they don't spend their time merely swanning around exotic places. However, the travel writers I know would never do anything else.

Don't forget that travel articles can be researched on your own doorstep. Few of us live more than a stone's throw away from delightful native countryside, historical towns and enchanting villages. What is commonplace for us can be fascinating for strangers. Take a good look round to see if your area offers something for the travel market.

I recommend photographers to read the excellent book *Photographing Historic Buildings* by Terry Buchanan, HMSO. It is full of advice for photographers in this field and is certain to stimulate ideas.

Before going anywhere which may have travel writing potential, do your research. Travel agencies, foreign tourist offices, embassies – all have potential. Research the books in the library for background information. Check the weather and political situation. You don't want to arrive when the climate is like a Turkish bath or during a guerilla war.

Next get your query letters off and get some commissions or at least some expressions of editorial interest.

Travel markets clearly have quite different needs in the information they wish to put over. A general magazine might only wish to know of your experiences on a visit to some unusual and exotic place. Another magazine might require detailed information which would help its readers to duplicate your holiday for themselves. How to get there –

where to stay – where to eat – what to eat – what to see – what to avoid – the advantages and the disadvantages. That type of magazine will want to know the snags and you must be honest.

The travel magazine demands that you be specific. Don't say 'The beach west of the town is beautiful.' People will ask, 'Beautiful for what, the sand, the casinos, the ice-cream or the view?' Say something like, 'The beach west of the town is my favourite. It is still relatively uncrowded although more people are discovering its attractions. The soft clean sand and the safe beach make it ideal for families with children. With trees only 200 metres from the water, there is welcome shade from the mid-day sun and a convenient place for picnics.'

Occasionally try to add something like, 'Don't park as soon as you reach the beach, but keep on until the road swings inland. Turn right here and park among the trees. You will find that you are uncrowded, closer to the beach and your car keeps cool all day.' Travel magazines love this confidential touch which not only shows you have been there, but makes the reader think that they are getting a little exclusive tip which gives them the edge on the other holiday-makers.

I used this hint of exclusive knowledge in the opening of an article called 'The magic of Idwal.'

Visitors to North Wales, travelling the A5 between Capel Curig and Bethesda, are captivated by the wild scenery, with the triple-headed heights of Tryfan on one hand and the waters of Llyn Ogwen on the other. At the head of the Nant Ffrancon Pass, they usually follow the road as it swings north and starts its descent to the sea, unaware that they have narrowly missed one of the finest jewels in Snowdonia – Cwm Idwal.

For the beginner, I would urge you to go only to a place which attracts you for its own sake, not to go because you think it has travel writing potential. Financially, you are unlikely to recoup the cost of your visit until you have experience and have your markets well tied up. So aim at enjoying your holiday and let your writing subsidise it. You never know where it might lead.

We write travel articles, but we never go to places which we are unlikely to enjoy. We get pleasure from our research and our legwork, but we are too fond of our creature comforts to head for the Amazon basin. Next month we are off to Sweden. 'In February?' our friends are saying. 'You must be crazy!' But we have our own ideas and they will probably get into print somewhere.

Chapter Thirteen

The Business side

The business side of writing is one aspect which few writers enjoy, but it is very important – even for beginners.

Keeping records
Keeping records of your work and its finances is common-sense, as well as being essential for tax purposes. Filing systems for facts, pictures, tear-sheets, typescripts and the other bits and pieces which writers collect, should be efficient and their contents easily retrievable. Efficiency saves time, which can be better spent writing.

Although one can use electronic filing systems associated with word-processors to store facts, the information still requires to be typed in. When, like us, you have over 30 years of accumulated material, it would probably take a year or more to get it loaded in the computer. We are storing selected new material on disc, but are resigned to keeping the old material as it is, on manual files.

Card index systems
A card index system is the best for most writers. Many years ago I had a printer cut up some of his surplus white card into 5 × 4 inch rectangles. They cost very little and I still have far more than I shall ever be able to use. This was much cheaper than buying lined filing-cards.

We have a number of large steel filing cabinets which readily take foolscap folders. In addition, we have several small steel cabinets which could carry several thousand filing cards. The cabinets were all bought very cheaply second-hand.

For our major specialist subjects we have 14 foolscap and A4 box-files, plus linen-reinforced A4 manila wallets. Both box-files and manila wallets stand on edge, filling several shelves of one study.

We are fortunate in having two studies, each with its own word-processor, enabling us to work independently.

Your precise method of filing is up to you, but be careful not to underestimate your ultimate needs. A simple way is to make up cards for every main subject. There can be several sub-headings under one main subject. For example, your card might be headed CHURCHES with sub-headings BRASSES, GRAVESTONES, EPITAPHS, ARCHITECT-URE, BELLS, CHURCHYARDS, etc.

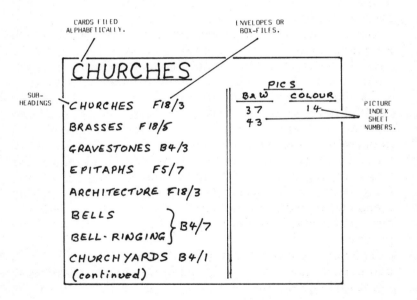

If a sub-heading becomes important, it can be given a card of its own. Good cross-referencing is essential for finding your way around your system easily.

The cards may then refer to numbered files. It is often

impossible to get every subject's sub-heading on to a card. However, you can put a more comprehensive index sheet inside the file itself.

Do keep filing systems up to date.

Storing photographs

Photographic negatives are kept in thin plastic divided wallets. The 35 mm films are cut into strips of six and filed seven strips to a wallet. The 120 film is cut into strips of three and filed four to a wallet. The wallets are held in strong ring-backed binders. Each wallet is identified numerically, each strip is lettered alphabetically and each negative numbered from left to right. Binders are labelled A1, A2 etc for 35 mm and B1, B2 for 120 files. So A1/17E4 leads me to binder A1 (for 35 mm), wallet 17, strip E, the fourth negative in the row. Every binder has its own index in the front and every negative is tied in to the main card index.

Contact sheets are also filed, plus any 10 × 8 prints which are either spare or have been returned by a magazine after use. The latter are useful for checking fine details of pictures which would be difficult to see in the negatives.

The bulkiness of 35 mm slides make them difficult to store easily. I have several systems, because the number of slides expands so rapidly and I just haven't made my mind up about which is the best way. I use straight plastic projector magazines which come in their own boxes, hold 100 slides per box and are surprisingly cheap. I have large rectangular filing boxes, which are bulky, expensive and not recommended. Many of my slides are stored in plastic wallets and also in the plastic boxes in which they are returned from processing.

The 6 × 6 slides are less robust than the mounted 35 mm and need extra care. They are all in thin plastic sleeves and are stored in wallets of twelve.

Business records

For your business records you need some basic record books. Try to keep these as simple as possible and only add to them if it appears to be essential. A manuscript book is necessary for booking your articles in and out, giving the date, the name of the article, who it went to and the outcome. A postage book is required for recording all postage, including SAE's and IRC's. A phone book for calls related to writing should be kept by the phone. It pays to have a simple timer which you start when the outgoing call is answered. You will be surprised how it all adds up.

Most important of all is the account book. This should be a large cash book. I use left-hand pages for expenditure and the right-hand pages for income.

For expenditure, I put the date of the expenditure or purchase, what it was and from where it was purchased. The amount is shown on the right-hand column of this page. I keep a separate column three-quarters of the way across the page for the amounts of purchases for which I shall claim the appropriate Capital Allowance.

On the right-hand page, I put the date, the magazine or publisher, the reason for payment and, in the last column, the amount. On this page I have another column three-quarters across and in this I record any expenses or part-expenses I have been paid.

I have a manila wallet in which all counterfoils and receipts are kept for that financial year.

You must record every payment made to you, however small. You must also record every expenditure on your writing activities, paper, ribbons, films, chemicals, pens, processing, paper clips, travelling for research and inter-viewing, subscriptions to professional societies, subscriptions to market research agencies, maintenance of typewriter or word-processor, insurance on photographic equipment etc.

What you should not record under your normal expenditure is new equipment – camera, word-processor, flash-gun etc. These must be shown in your Capital Allowance column.

Tax returns
Your Income Tax return from writing will be under Schedule D and should be made to your usual tax office. Don't be tempted to brush this aside and say, 'I don't make anything

much, so it isn't worthwhile.' If someone had given me the following advice many years ago, I would have saved a great deal of money.

If you are not earning very much, then you are probably writing at a loss and, if so, you must record it. Type out a simple tax return in the form of a balance sheet which you can copy from your account book. Make a note of any expenditure for which you can claim Capital Allowance. Show your loss clearly. It can easily be several hundreds of pounds.

Write a covering letter to your tax inspector, explaining that you are trying to establish a career as a writer and ask for your loss to be recorded. Under normal circumstances it will not be set against your tax liability from other sources, but will be ultimately set against your future profits from writing. These losses can accrue and can prove most valuable when you move into profit, ensuring tax-free earnings until the losses are absorbed. This advice could save you several thousands of pounds.

Currently, you can claim 25% Capital Allowance for any new equipment purchased during the financial year. The balance, namely 75%, is carried forward and 25% of this balance may be claimed in subsequent years. In any financial year in which a loss is made, Capital Allowance may be carried forward to offset future profits.

Cars are a special case of their own and the simplest thing is to record every mile travelled on writing business and claim a mileage rate. This rate can be obtained from the Automobile Association for the current year, if you state the size of your car.

You can claim as an expenditure for tax purposes, the partial use of the room you use for your writing. This can include a proportion of the heating, lighting, maintenance and insurance of the property. This proportion should be agreed with your tax inspector. You should not claim for a proportion of the rates, nor should you claim for the exclusive use of a room for writing. To do so would run the risk of having part of the property considered business premises and therefore liable to Capital Gains Tax if the house were ultimately sold.

Tax evasion is illegal, so declare every penny earned. Tax avoidance is legal, so record every penny spent. I am meticulous about my returns. I have been called twice for interviews with my tax inspector over my writing returns. Fortunately, I was able to prove my points and my returns were fully accepted. Had I been less than honest, I am sure the interviews would have been a very uncomfortable business.

Make sure you keep copies of all correspondence on tax matters and copies of all returns.

I am not a tax consultant. Also, tax regulations change all the time. For these reasons I offer the above information in good faith and as it applies to me. I caution you to verify the application of any of the above points to your own personal circumstances. The ultimate responsibility for your tax return is your own.

Chapter Fourteen

The way ahead

At some stage, most writers reach the apparent impasse when they ask, 'Where am I going wrong?' It is at this point that the limitations of all books on writing become apparent. There is no feedback, no interchange of ideas, no opportunity for the reader to challenge the author's concepts. Most sorely missed is the expert finger pointing out that over-looked shortcoming.

Editors rarely offer constructive criticism, although it does sometimes happen. More often, they are far too busy.

Writing is like so many skills. Some little thing is going wrong, but we lack the objectivity or experience to see it for ourselves. We are like the golfers who are unable to get their swing right, then, after half an hour with the professional, they get the shrewd tip which puts them right.

All writers benefit from expert criticism. Established writers need it to prevent complacency and to get them out of the occasional rut. It also helps them to polish their style and sharpen their perspective. Beginners need it to stop them wandering down fruitless cul-de-sacs and to point the way out of their confidence-sapping rejections.

Writers' Circles
Writers' Circles can be very helpful and there are a great number of them around. Their quality varies considerably. Many are excellent, but some are self-congratulatory meetings over a cup of tea, where too many members are afraid to criticise honestly and unable to accept criticism

when it is offered. In others there may be no writer experienced enough to criticise effectively.

Fortunately, there are a good number of established writers who will give up their precious writing time to go to Writers' Circles to speak, to hear readings and also to adjudicate in competitions. It is well worth taking advantage of these sessions.

A list of about 300 names and addresses of Writers' Circles in England, Scotland and Wales is available from Jill Dick, Oldacre, Horderns Park Road, Chapel-en-le-Frith, Derbyshire, SK12 6SY.

Writing courses

Correspondence courses may have some merit, but I have yet to be convinced of it. Generally, they are expensive and, from examples I have seen and from my own experience, the criticisms are often unimpressive. However, I don't like to generalise and there may well be courses which could be useful, but I have yet to find them.

I am convinced that residential courses are the best way of getting your writing kinks straightened out, but they must include the opportunity for counselling with someone who specialises in your field. It is of limited use to go to a novelist for advice on articles or to an article-writer for help with short stories. Many writers have a touch of the Jack-of-all trades about them, but the good ones specialise. They may all be good at handling words, but on at least one point they tend to fall down – they only know about their own markets. Remember, market knowledge is vital for article-writing success.

Even on residential courses there is some mediocrity. A good test of a tutor is to try to discover the markets for which he writes. If he is a 'penny-a-liner', as they used to call them, writing for too many publications which pay £25 per thousand and less at present rates, then be careful. Rest assured he would write for the more prestigious markets if he could. That is not to say that he may not be able to give you considerable help to reach his own standards.

Some tutors give their students their all – personal

guidance from before breakfast until late into the night – chats over meals and in the bar. A number of tutors invite manuscripts to be sent to them in advance for criticism and discussion on the course. This is a great bonus for the student, but hard work for the tutor. Anyone who has an opportunity of attending a Novel Writing course, tutored by Dianne Doubtfire, will have an outstanding example of the tremendous amount of worthwhile information a dedicated tutor can pack into one weekend. Her courses are hard work, but well worth watching out for, if you aspire to novel writing.

Sadly, some courses are easy rides for both tutors and students – delightful weekends maybe, but of little real practical help.

My wife, Molly, and I tutor article-writing courses at a number of colleges and we find them very rewarding. They have made us many good friends and some of our students have become highly successful writers. This is to their credit, not ours. We have merely pointed the way, they did all the hard work which brought success.

Our personal favourite is the five-day course. Writers are invited to submit work in advance if they wish. The first lectures are instructions in the basics. Then the students are given a choice of carefully selected projects which may include local research, interviewing, photography and other skills, according to their inclinations. Shy ones go in pairs. The material obtained is written up and knocked into shape, with guidance along the way. Happily, quite a lot of this work is ultimately sold.

This is the type of course which I recommend beginners to look out for. It is infinitely better than those which rely on lectures and discussion alone. Molly and I run such courses fairly regularly at Maryland College, Woburn, Milton Keynes, MK17 9JD. Details may be obtained from the Principal.

The details of adult residential courses, both weekends and longer, are published twice-yearly from The National Institute of Adult Continuing Education, 19B, De Montfort St., Leicester, LE1 7GE.

The Writers' Summer School

The Mecca of all writers in Britain is The Writers' Summer School, which I have already mentioned. It is held at Swanwick in Derbyshire. It runs from Saturday to the following Friday and is held annually in mid-August. Details are obtainable from the Secretary – Mrs Philippa Boland, The Red House, Mardens Hill, Crowborough, Sussex, TN6 1XN. Although the conference centre accommodates about 350 writers, demand far exceeds the places available.

In 1987 a similar activity was launched at Caerleon in Gwent. Called Writers' Holiday, it is achieving a happy balance between holiday, lecture, discussion and coursework. It is held in July and the fees in 1991 were £135, full board, from Sunday to Friday. The administrator is Mrs Anne Hobbs, 30 Pant Road, Newport, Gwent, NP9 5PR.

Writing is a lonely business. So it is a valuable spin-off from courses to meet other writers, and share their hopes, problems and even despair. Such exchanges are both reassuring and therapeutic. You will also find that most writers are generous people, sharing knowledge, details of markets and other guidance which is invaluable to us all in our early stages.

Although hard work plays a very large part in our prospects of success, it is the belief in our ultimate ability to succeed which is vital. A negative outlook shows up in our work. I have even seen it in a writer's query letter to an editor, 'I don't suppose you would be interested in . . .'

The will to succeed singles out the winners from the faint-hearted writers who falter to a halt after the first one or two rejection slips.

If you have read this book right through to the end, then I believe you can succeed and you should believe it too. You must generate the self-confidence by telling yourself that you *will* succeed. Keep on saying it until you truly believe it.

Finally, this book is only a series of signposts. The hard work is up to you. Go to it!